PLATO'S 'REPUBLIC'

TO

THE HONOURABLE FRANCES P. BOLTON

'There are to be men and women guardians
with their work in common'

PLATO'S REPUBLIC

EDITED AND TRANSLATED BY

I. A. RICHARDS

CAMBRIDGE
AT THE UNIVERSITY PRESS
1966

PUBLISHED BY
THE SYNDICS OF THE CAMBRIDGE UNIVERSITY PRESS

Bentley House, 200 Euston Road, London, N.W.1
American Branch: 32 East 57th Street, New York, N.Y. 10022
West African Office: P.M.B. 5181, Ibadan, Nigeria

Printed in Great Britain at the University Printing House, Cambridge
(Brooke Crutchley, University Printer)

LIBRARY OF CONGRESS CATALOGUE
CARD NUMBER: 66-10544

INTRODUCTION

We should ask today of *The Republic* a question of which Plato would have much approved. He asked it himself of Homer and came up with a surprisingly negative answer: Out with it. He found Homer, and the poetry deriving from Homer, responsible for much that was wrong with Greece in his time. It would not be hard to draw up a set of charges accusing Plato, and *The Republic* in particular, of having contributed much to our political and moral troubles. In fact many sprightly critics have done so. Our question, of course, is, Why read it? A present-day Plato would not allow us to be content with the ordinary answers. Let us look at a few of these first before considering what Plato might accept as a good answer.

We could say, Read it because it has been one of the half-dozen most influential books in the history of writing. That is so. It has been, for thought and institutions in the western tradition, more or less what Mencius has been for China, the Vedas and Upanishads for India, the Sutras for the Buddhist world, the Koran for Islam, the Old Testament for Judaism, or the Bible for Christendom. It has been a major instrument in shaping a culture. Directly and, still more, through the countless minds it has persuaded or *antagonized*, it has entered into the very design and fabric of every Western man's thought and will and feeling. Emerson lent *The Republic* to a Yankee farmer who after reading it through remarked, 'That man has a great number of my ideas'.

Another reply might be: Read it because it is the founding document of the academic way of study. It is that. Plato is believed to have written it not long after he had planned and opened his Academy, about 388 B.C. That cult-society of teachers and scholars, the first university, survived till 529 A.D., longer than even the universities of Paris and Oxford (founded in the twelfth century) have yet endured. Much in it, especially in Book VII, is an outline for a programme of studies for members of the

Academy, with reflections on the spirit in which they were to be pursued.

A third answer could be: If you know *The Republic* well, countless passages in great literature, taken for granted in the discussion of the most diverse subjects, become easily intelligible. You see what they are about. Without that you have to guess and are likely to guess wrong. Illustrations might be endless. I will pick one in which a very central thing in Plato is applied to a deeply concerning topic. In John Donne's poem, *The Exstasie*, at its climax come the lines:

> So must pure lovers souls descend
> T'affections, and to faculties,
> Which sense may reach and apprehend,
> Else a great Prince in prison lies.
> To our bodies turn we then . . . . (65–9)

The poem has been discussing, with two lovers speaking together as one, what place the body has in love. At this point it uses Plato's account of the three parts of the soul: the best part, that which knows and loves knowledge; the spirited, executive part which helps the best part and loves honour; and the third part, the desires and appetites, the senses (see 435–44,[1] pp. 79–83 below; 580–1, pp. 166–7 below; 587–9, pp. 169–71 below). It says that *the great Prince* (the whole soul with its power and duty to rule) will remain *in prison* unless *pure lovers souls* come down from their exstasie, their transcendental detachment, to the feelings and the motions of the will (the sentiments, we might say) and get *them* to control and direct the senses, appetites and desires. The spirited part of the mind can handle sense (and sense can take in what spirit directs); but knowledge by itself cannot manage sense, nor will sense listen to it. The intermediary role of the affections and the faculties (which form the Lion that comes between the Man and the Many-headed beast: (588–90)) is Plato's invention and so is the image of the prison-house (515, 580): the fate of the Man if the Lion does not support him.

[1] These numbers (usually printed in brackets) refer to pages of the Stephanus edition of 1578.

Interpretations that are given of these lines (and of the whole poem as a result) by readers who have not recognized what *The Republic* is doing in it can be too queer to be believed.

A fourth answer might be: Read it because it first formulates for discussion a theory of the aims and methods of education. It both sets up a pattern for what the educator should hope to produce and offers strong views on how best to work towards it. Naturally, both ends and means have been criticized, not less today than in past centuries. On the other hand, they have been surprisingly often followed (in various adaptations): in the British institution, the 'Public School', for example, as training the future administrator. Not a few high Civil Service Officials have been known to murmur, and with some justice: 'We are the Philosopher Kings, alas, forced back down into the Cave!' (see 473, p. 97 below, and 520, p. 128 below).

Which leads us to a fifth answer: Read *The Republic* because Plato there founds political science. He supplies a series of diagram-like type-specimens and case histories which nobody concerned with what governments may be like can find matched elsewhere. Naturally again, his pages have been a perennial battleground. It is fashionable at present to call him a Fascist, yet his sketch of the *tyrant* (Book IX) reads as if it were a first-hand exposure of Hitler. The aim and effect of the book as a whole is to set up the very concepts which can best protect us from mutual interference and oppression. Without them we should be defenceless—against the manipulations of a blind social science, for example (506), and its servants among educators. We need such defences increasingly, active and alert in as many minds as possible. What was written for aristocrats in a city-state has become the primer for world citizenship.

His importance as founder of theoretical politics is equalled for psychology, for ethics, for theory of knowledge, for metaphysics, for most of the facets or aspects of philosophy, to use that most disputable of all key words. Whitehead observed that the history of western philosophy might be most compendiously described as a series of footnotes to footnotes...to Plato. The better anyone knows that history (and Plato) the more he is apt to agree. Whitehead, incidentally, when he was chairman of a score of committees of London University—to and from whose meetings he would travel on top of a bus—used to make a practice of seating some great intellectual ghost beside him: an Aristotle, a Dante, a Newton, a Voltaire...to whom he would explain whatever the streets might offer to interest his companion. The only ghost, he told me, he would never dare invite was Plato's. It would have asked too many paralysing questions.

None of these reasons for reading *The Republic* would have satisfied Plato. They are true, no doubt, in a sense, but not in the sense he cared most about. 'True' is inevitably a most tricky and misleading word here. *The Republic*, above and beyond all else that it tries to do, tries to help us with this word:

GLAUCON. Who then are the true philosophers?
SOCRATES. Those who are in love with seeing what is true.

(475 E, p. 99 below)

This is in part a provocative spelling-out by Socrates of the etymology of *philosopher* (Gr. *philosophos*: a lover of *sophia*, wisdom); but he knows as he teases Glaucon that the rest of the discussion recounted in *The Republic* is required if these two uses of *true* are to be kept to their proper work, that is, be *justly* comprehended.

Immediately before this Socrates has been saying: 'Whoever has a taste for every sort of knowledge, and desires to learn and never has enough of it, may be named a philosopher' (475 C). This omnivorous appetite for studies is a mark of the philosophic nature, but there is more to it:

SOCRATES. You have heard times enough that the greatest thing to learn is the idea of good through which, only, just things and all the rest become useful and do good. And now I am almost certain you see that this is what I am going to talk about and that I am going to say, moreover, that we haven't enough knowledge of it. Even though we had ever so much knowledge of other things, that would do us no good. Would owning every other thing profit us if we didn't own anything good? (505 B)

It is characteristic of Plato that he makes his Socrates—as he nears this culminating point, this first principle on which all else depends—hold back and refuse to admit that he knows. Whether this was characteristic of Socrates himself too, no one can say for certain. It seems likely that it was.

In any case Plato's own careful avoidance of any claim to certainty, coming always exactly where his students most want him to claim it, puts this question, Why read him?, in a peculiar light. It suggests that the string of 'ordinary answers' I have been running through would seem to him to leave out what most matters and to be more concerned with 'other things' than with that from which such 'other things,' other sorts of knowledge among them, derive their values.

If we call this source of values, as he does, *wisdom*, we can answer our key question in what may seem a very simple fashion: we read him to gain wisdom. But then we have the task of learning, of recognizing for ourselves, what this unique thing 'wisdom' may be.

This is not a matter of telling ourselves, or telling others, what it is, of giving the formulation that Plato so resolutely, so constantly refrained from offering. Formulation, he had learned—very likely from Socrates—gets in the way here. The task is much more one of remembering how or where to look, how to turn the mind's eye in another direction:

SOCRATES. Education is not truly what some of its professors say it is. They say they are able to put knowledge into a soul which hasn't got it—as if they were putting sight into blind eyes.

GLAUCON. They do say so.

SOCRATES. But our argument points to this: the natural power to learn lives in the soul and is like an eye which might not be turned from the dark without a turning round of the whole body. The instrument of knowledge has to be turned round, and with it the whole soul, from the things of becoming to the things of being, till the soul is able, by degrees, to support the light of true being and can look at the brightest. And this, we say, is the good? (518, p. 126 below)[1]

[1] 'Nothing is wanted but the eye, which is the light of this house, the light which is the eye of this soul. This *seeing* light, this *enlightening* eye, is Reflection. It is more, indeed, than is ordinarily meant by that word; but it is what

'The *whole* soul', be it noted. As Cornford well put it: 'To achieve wisdom would be to achieve human perfection, well-being, happiness.'[1]

This contrast between 'the things of becoming and the things of being' is often made to seem more difficult than it need be, or it is given the wrong kind of difficulty, by being treated as a theory—the theory of Ideas—instead of being taken simply as an evident familiar fact or power which we all use and depend on.

Take any sort of things: letter A's for example. We meet with endless numbers and varieties of them: A, *A*, a, *a*, **a**, . . . etc. They can be of all sizes and be as various as the printers' founts or as handwritings will let them be. Put them under the microscope and no two of them, we see, are the same. But instead of talking of A's we can say 'the letter A' and agree that there can be endless different instances of *it*. We can divide these instances up: into printed and typewritten and handwritten, into capital and lower-case, legible and illegible...and so on and on. All this we know as a set of familiar facts about which there will be no disagreement whatsoever.

This is the contrast between the world of Becoming and the world of Being. Letter A's, as instances of *the letter A*, belong to the world of Becoming. They are events. They come and go. They are many. The letter A, on the other hand, does not come and it does not go. And it is one. It is not an event; it is a Form or Idea. An Idea or Form is not a happening in a mind (or a head). It is an object which certain happenings in minds can be OF. As a Form (or Idea, or object of thought), it has an entirely different status from that of any instance of it and from any event in anyone's mind, any thinking of it. Two different events in two minds can be *of* the same object. But two people cannot strictly see the same instances of it; their eyes are different. We

a *Christian* ought to mean by it and to know, too, whence it first came, and still continues to come—of what light even this light is but a reflection. This, too, is THOUGHT, and all thought is but unthinking that does not flow out of this, or tend towards it' (S. T. Coleridge, *Aids to Reflection*, Aphorism IX).

[1] F. M. Cornford, *Republic*, Introduction, p. xxiv.

can see, we can write, we can cross out letter A's. But we never meet, and can do nothing to the letter A or to any other member of the world of Being.

Consider lines, circles and triangles now. The lines of geometry belong to the world of Being; those the geometer may draw to the world of Becoming. He uses them to help him to think about Forms—in the world of Being. Forms themselves are not able to be seen or drawn, but they can be thought of.

Another way which Plato uses of describing this contrast is as between the visible and the intelligible. This adds another point we can all confirm. What is intelligible belongs to *an order*. A circle is intelligible. As a Form the points on the circumference are at equal distances from the centre. There is nothing accidental about this. But any visible actual instance of a circle will be found, if we care to examine it closely, to be all accidents; the parts of its circumference occur where the point of the pencil travelling over the irregular surface of the paper happened to go. Any *account*, however, that we may attempt to give of these accidents must be given by using, as best we can, the intelligible order. The world of Becoming is indescribable—except through the Forms (Ideas) of the world of Being.

In setting up this contrast, Plato, for the most part in *The Republic*, is doing no more than recognizing something that is inescapably necessary for intelligibility, namely order. It is necessary for any communication too. And there is nothing in that, so far, to cause difficulty. But the Academy and notably Aristotle—who joined it at seventeen and stayed till Plato's death, twenty years later—introduced, through efforts to explain and develop the contrast theoretically, a multiplying swarm of invitations to misunderstanding and dissension which has haunted technical or academic philosophy ever since. It is arguable that there is nothing useful that any theoretical explanation or development here can do.

One outcome of the contrast has been of immense importance. The Forms are unchanging; it is their duty, their work and business to be constant as maintaining the order ruled over by the supreme Idea, the Good. But the events in the world of Becoming are inherently changeful and the changes that matter most to most men are births and deaths. It is not strange then that the concern of the soul with the world of Being should have been at once connected with arguments in favour of the immortality of the soul. Note how Socrates suddenly surprises Glaucon (608 E, p. 184 below) with his conviction on this. The arguments he uses there have not in general convinced others. Far more influential has been his view (611) that the soul can become *like* the objects it cares for, the ideal company it keeps. This is the picture we recognize of our souls. These passages should be read together with Socrates' conversation on his last afternoon while waiting to drink the hemlock. (*Phaedo*, 81, *Why So, Socrates?*, p. 47.) It seems in both at times as though the soul's true business were to win immortality—in which most fail (534 D, p. 137 below). The dialogue form—by giving any such affirmations to Socrates and at a particular turn only of the discussion—protects Plato from having to speak with over-confidence himself.

The dramatic handling in *The Republic* (as in earlier dialogues) has other great advantages. It allows Plato to sketch, to anticipate, to return to amplify—after an interval in which doubts and qualifications have had time to take effect. Thus Book I is essentially a 'curtain-raiser' only preparing for what is to come. Many, however, have thrown the book down in dissatisfaction before reaching the main action at the opening of Book II. Some of this Plato meant his readers to feel. Thrasymachus *does* give up too easily. Socrates' arguments *are* like a fencer's tricks. On the other hand this preliminary conversation outlines the positions to be developed later: among them Socrates' extraordinary view, never uttered by any before him, that it is never right to harm anyone, however much of an enemy he may be. And we only realize the full significance of Thrasymachus when we come to the portrait of the tyrant in Book IX.

Again, as Plato pursues the great parallel between a society and a mind (CAPITAL LETTERS to be compared with lower-case) we do well to note that Socrates warns Glaucon—who with Adeimantus was surely the very best audience any man ever had—that 'we won't ever get a true answer to all this by the ways we have been using' (435 D), referring him to the longer, harder treatment that studies in the Academy (504–41) were to be aimed at. Meanwhile the parallel, the analogy between a State and an individual mind, enables Plato to say more than a little about the inner politics of the soul and much that the longer, harder way is even today still barely approaching. We should not overlook that at one of the high points of the book (533, p. 135 below) comes this:

SOCRATES. My dear Glaucon, you will not be able to come farther with me, however willing I might be. If I were able, I would give you no longer any comparison, picture or parable, but the truth itself, as I see it, though if rightly or not is not for me to say.

To give that 'truth itself' in due time is to be the task of *dialectic*.

This word, dialectic, thanks to vagaries in philosophy, among which those of Hegel and Marx are best known, has become dangerously misleading here. For Plato it stands in contrast to *eristic* or word-fighting, the art of the disputant who is arguing for victory, not for truth (454, p. 88 below). Dialectic is a very different art of discourse, the art of making clear in any discussion what the participants are really saying and thinking—all with reference to the prime diagram of the Divided Line (509) and its hierarchic proportion.

Picturing : Belief :: Understanding : Reason

Socrates' estimate as to how long an adequate discussion of *that* would take (534) has been amply confirmed by the history of philosophy. It is not nearly finished yet. Some would say that it is barely begun.

Plato believed deeply in the merits of *discussion*, joint endeavour by more than one mind, as a means of examining any question.

He even goes so far, in his *Phaedrus* (274–5), as to make Socrates attack writing because written words have no power to defend themselves from misunderstanding. Especially is this so of philosophic terms:

SOCRATES. When one says 'silver' or 'iron' we all understand the same thing?

PHAEDRUS. Of course.

SOCRATES. What if he says 'justice' or 'goodness'? Don't we go different ways and disagree with one another and with ourselves? (263 A)

The remedy he proposes is the art 'of perceiving and bringing together in one idea the scattered particulars...and of dividing things where the *natural* joints are without breaking any part like a bad carver' (265 E). 'I myself', Socrates says, 'am a lover of these processes of dividing and bringing together...and if any other man is able to see how things can be *naturally* collected into one and divided into many, I walk in his footsteps as if he were a god. Those who can do this I call—rightly or wrongly, God knows—*dialecticians*' (266 B). If our answer to 'Why read *The Republic*?' were that we could learn from it how to improve in this art, Plato would have accepted that as *part* of a good answer. Dialogue and dialectic for him go together, the participating minds redressing one another's mistakings, as our two eyes see better than either can alone.

A few remarks on some distortions in *The Republic* which most readers notice may round off this Introduction. Plato grew up in a grim period of the decline of Athens, in a world of misdirected ambition and political breakdown. His knowledge of what civil war can do made him value strong and stable government beyond measure. He had felt the duty and the impossibility, the futility for him, of playing a part in politics. Some of his descriptions of the temptations of a young philosopher (494, p. 108 below; 538, p. 139 below) might well be autobiographical. But, as a young man (under thirty when his adored teacher, Socrates, was executed), he was without much talent for 'seeing in the dark' (520 C, p. 128 below), the darkness of political action. To have been effective in his Athens he would have had to learn the management of the great beast (493, p. 107 below) and the art of how to seize the helm (488 B, p. 104 below). Later, when he had been disappointed, and worse, in his hopes from a field-experiment in Sicily, he developed the preternatural imaginative acuteness in diagnosis displayed in Books VIII and IX. And his ambitions revived with the founding of the Academy. Are not reflective educators under the spell of the most exacting ambition there is—the remaking of man?

'There are two ways in which our eyes (the eye of the body and the eye of the mind alike) may be troubled: when they change over from the light to the dark and from the dark to the light' (518). The two greatest defects in *The Republic* may reasonably be regarded as due to bedazzlement by sudden increase of light. They are (1) the lengths to which Plato pushes his prescription: 'One man—one job; one faculty—one programme', and (2) his Tolstoy-like rejection of poetry and art. Both, it may be suggested, are cases of blinding by new illumination.

(1) Dazzled by his discovery of Justice as Order: as everything in its due place doing there the work it is *for*, he over-applies it. He loses sight of the widely recognized fact that an expert in any art usually needs experience of the creative effort in other arts than his own if he is to remain balanced and do his best work.

(2) Plato invites the poets to refute his charges (607), if they can, in any verse they please, and lovers of poetry and the arts may do the same in prose. Aristotle's *Poetics* is an early retort and answers in verse and prose continue to be written—by good Platonists who are good poets above all; Dante, Spenser, Sidney, Shakespeare, Donne, Shelley and Yeats are among them. The reply is that poetry and the arts can and do, in their own ways, represent the Forms:

The gathered rays that are reality[1]

[1] Shelley, *Prometheus Unbound*, Act III, Scene iii, l. 53.

and that to do so is to be 'not only delightful but useful in ordering government and man's life'. A remarkable amount of great poetry has, in fact, been devoted to this theme. Poetry, as Shelley claimed, is the unacknowledged legislation of mankind.[1] Plato in Book x is doing as bad carvers do, hacking through parts. We may imagine Socrates in Elysium congratulating him for having provoked such magnificent rejoinders. And we will forgive both errors if we realize how new and overpowering at first his vision of *sophia*

> Apparelled in celestial light[2]

must have been.

Plato was writing in a reactionary spirit at a time when the independent city-state in Greece—though it did not know this—was doomed. The version in your hand is written to be read by newcomers to Plato's territory at a time when, it is probable, nations as sovereign states are out of date. Many of the new nations have inherited political conditions and political problems remarkably like those which forced Plato to look to a fundamental reconstruction of education as man's best hope. One of the fundamentals which Plato stresses (e.g. 462, 590E) is the need for common experience, experience shared by as many as possible, if common action, based on agreement as to ends and means, is to be developed. In such common experience man's conception of his own nature, of what he should be and of how he may best attempt to become so, holds the central place. This is the theme of *The Republic* throughout:

> What is there in thee, Man, that can be known?[3]

as Coleridge asked. It is not an accident that Plato's account of man as an individual and as a political being should have spread

[1] *The Defence of Poetry*, final paragraph.

[2] Wordsworth, *Intimations of Immortality*.

[3] 'Self-Knowledge.' Coleridge on Plato: 'This plank from the wreck of Paradise thrown on the shores of idolatrous Greece' (*Aids to Reflection*, p. xxxii). More perhaps than any other thinker, Coleridge illustrates the imitation Greek epigram: 'Wherever I go in my mind, I meet Plato on his way back.'

as it has. Werner Jaeger was perhaps not unjust when he wrote: 'The greatest invention of the Greeks was man.' Plato's account is, at least, the only one that takes up the problem of self-government within a community and the cultivation of temperance (*sophrosyne*) in such a way that peoples of diverse cultures, in different stages of political development, can study it together. As such *The Republic* is the indispensable instrument for the cultivation of common understanding in the most important matters. May this version—in an English which I have made as simple, as suited to newcomers in such studies, as loyalty to the meaning allowed—serve this cause. For, as Socrates reminds Glaucon (608, p. 184 below), 'Much turns, more than we are conscious of, on a man's becoming good or bad.'

BOOK I

At the opening of The Republic, SOCRATES *has gone down, with Plato's brother* GLAUCON, *to the harbour near Athens, the Peiraeus, to make his prayer to the goddess. He is starting back on his five-mile walk to Athens, when some friends see him and take him to the house of his old friend* CEPHALUS *for talk. Among the group there are* POLEMARCHUS, *son of Cephalus,* ADEIMANTUS, *Glaucon's brother, and* THRASYMACHUS, *a noted Sophist.*

To Socrates Cephalus seemed much older than when he last saw him years before. He was seated with a wreath on his head, for he had been making the offerings. They joined him and took their places in a circle about him.

CEPHALUS. You are not often here, Socrates. You don't come down to see us. That is not right. If I were still strong enough to walk up to Athens there would be no need. But, as it is, you will have to come here. For, let me say this, as the pleasures of the body get less, the stronger the desire for good talk becomes. So don't say 'No', but come, make this house your own, and keep these young men company.

SOCRATES. Yes, Cephalus, and I like talking with the very old too. For to me they have gone ahead in the journey which we also may have to go. What is the road like, rough and hard or smooth and easy? How does it seem to you? Is living harder near the end, or what account do you give of it?

CEPHALUS. Certainly, Socrates, I will say how it seems to (329) me. A group of us old men frequently meet, 'Like to like', as the saying is, and most of us make a sad to-do about our young days that were and about the pleasures of wine, woman, and song that have long gone from us. By their account, they are hardly living at all now. But to me, Socrates, they don't get at the true cause. For if being old were the cause, I and all the other old men would have the same feelings. But this is not my experience or that of others of my friends. I well remember how Sophocles, when he was very old, answered the question, 'What about love now, Sophocles, are you still the man you were?' 'Peace,' he said, 'how happy am I to be free from that tyrant of my earlier days.' I often think of his words and they seem to me as good now as when he said them. For certainly with old age comes a great sense of being quiet and free. Men's regrets, Socrates, and all their protests about cold-hearted relations and so on, come not from their years but from their make-up; for to anyone who is naturally well balanced, age is no great weight. But to men of the opposite sort, being young and being old are equally causes of trouble.

SOCRATES. I doubt if many, Cephalus, will agree with you; they will say it is not your outlook but your wealth which makes you take your years lightly. Money is a great comforter.

CEPHALUS. You are right, and there is something in what they say. Not, however, very much. The answer that Themistocles gave is to the point here. When a man from the little island of Seriphus said to him that his great name was not of his own making but came from his being an (330) Athenian, he said, 'If you were from Athens and I from Seriphus, no one would have heard of either of us!' The same may be said of the poor who take their years hard. If you are poor—however good you may be—old age isn't easy; but a bad man, however much wealth he has, will never be at peace with himself.

SOCRATES. But, Cephalus, did your money come to you from your father or did you make it yourself?

CEPHALUS. Did I make it myself, Socrates? Why, as a money-maker I come half way between my father and his father. For my father had a great amount of money from his, but he let much of it go, and I will be happy if my sons get from me what I got or a little more.

SOCRATES. The reason for my question is that I see you do not care overmuch about money, and that is generally a mark of those who have not made it themselves. Those who have are hard to talk to because they seem unwilling to value anything but money.

CEPHALUS. That is so.

SOCRATES. It is indeed. But may I ask this: What do you take to be the greatest good which you have had from your money?

CEPHALUS. Something which others, it may be, would not readily believe. But let me say this to you, Socrates. When a man sees himself to be near death, fears and cares come into his mind which he never had before. Stories of the other country to which he goes after death, and of the punishments there given, were things to be laughed at earlier. But now he is troubled by the thought that they may be true. Because he is feeble with years or, maybe, because, being nearer to that other place, he has a clearer view of it, fears and doubts come thickly upon him and he thinks of the wrongs he may have done to others. And if he has a very black record, he will start up in fear again and again, like a baby in his sleep, and be full of heavy thoughts of things to come. But to him who is (331) conscious of no ill-doing, and only of living through his days as a just man, 'Sweet hope,' as Pindar says, 'that chiefly rules the changeful minds of men, is the kind nurse of his last days.' And a beautiful saying it is, Socrates. And the best thing about money—I do not say to every man but to a good man—is that with it he has had no cause to do wrong to others, consciously or unconsciously; and so when he goes from this earth, he has no fears about offerings to the gods which he has not made, or about debts to other men which he has not given back. Money is a great help to this peace of mind through justice. It has other uses. But after balancing them all, I say this, of all the great good things it may do for men, this to a man of good sense is by far the greatest.

SOCRATES. Well said, Cephalus; but as to this very thing, justice, that we are talking about, is it no more than saying what is true and giving back whatever has been given to us? Or may these same acts be sometimes just and sometimes unjust? I take it everyone would agree that if a friend gave you a knife to take care of and later went out of his mind and came back for the knife, it would be wrong to give it back to him. That would not be just. And we would not say only what is true to a man in that condition.

CEPHALUS. You are right.

SOCRATES. Then justice isn't simply saying what is true and paying back our debts?

POLEMARCHUS. Ah, but it is, Socrates, if we are to believe Simonides.

CEPHALUS. Very well, Polemarchus, I make over my side of the discussion to you. It is time for me to be present at the offerings.

SOCRATES. It seems that all your goods are coming to Polemarchus.

CEPHALUS. Indeed they are. (*Exit Cephalus.*)

SOCRATES. What was it Simonides said?

POLEMARCHUS. That it is just to give every man what he should get.

SOCRATES. Simonides ought to know, for he is a wise man and inspired. But what do you think he meant? You, no doubt, know, but I don't.

POLEMARCHUS. Simonides thinks we ought to do our friends good, not evil.

SOCRATES. And how about our enemies?

POLEMARCHUS. Why, we should do to them what they deserve —evil, not good.

SOCRATES. (334) And by friends do you mean those who are or those who seem to be friends? And by enemies, those who are or those who seem so?

POLEMARCHUS. Don't we like those we think are for us and dislike those we think are against us?

SOCRATES. And don't we make mistakes in all that?

POLEMARCHUS. Of course we do.

what to do to friends

SOCRATES. And when we do? Would it then be just to do good to our enemies and evil to our friends?

POLEMARCHUS. Socrates! Something has gone wrong. Had we not better say that it is the good man who is our friend and the bad man who is our enemy?

SOCRATES. You said it was just to do good to friends and evil to enemies. Do you want to say now that it is just to do good to a friend, *if he is good*, and to do evil to an enemy, *if he is evil*?

POLEMARCHUS. Right! That is the way to put it.

SOCRATES. So it is just for a good man to harm people?

POLEMARCHUS. Of course it is. A man ought to harm bad people who are his enemies.

SOCRATES. Tell me, when horses are harmed does that make them better or worse, *as horses*?

POLEMARCHUS. Worse, of course.

SOCRATES. That is so too, with dogs, isn't it?

POLEMARCHUS. Yes it is.

SOCRATES. And with men? It is *as men* that they are harmed?

POLEMARCHUS. Certainly.

SOCRATES. Is not their justness the very thing that makes men human?

POLEMARCHUS. I have to say 'Yes' to that too.

SOCRATES. Don't you have to agree then that men who are harmed become less just?

POLEMARCHUS. So it seems.

SOCRATES. Then do just men, by being just, make other men unjust? Can a good man, by his goodness, make men bad?

POLEMARCHUS. No, that's not possible.

SOCRATES. Heat does not make things colder; dryness does not make things wetter. Does goodness make things worse? It is not the work of the just man, Polemarchus, to make anyone worse. That is what the unjust man does, isn't it?

POLEMARCHUS. Socrates, I think you are quite right.

SOCRATES. So whoever said that the way to be just is to harm our enemies and do good to our friends was not a wise man.

For if this was what he meant, it isn't true. It is clear to us now that it is never just to harm anyone.

POLEMARCHUS. You are right.

SOCRATES. I think that saying about justice wasn't from Simonides or from any other wise man, but from some Xerxes, some rich and powerful tyrant with a great idea of his own greatness.

THRASYMACHUS. What sort of nonsense is all this you have been talking? Why are you playing with one another so like a sweet pair of 'yes-men'? If you truly have any desire, Socrates, to know what justice is, don't limit yourself to questions. Let us have your answers as well. You know very well, don't you, that it is much easier to ask questions than to answer them? And please don't say that justice is what we have to do, or something like that, or that it is what is helpful, or in agreement with our needs, or what gives us profit, or what it's in our interest to do, or anything of that sort. That sort of answer won't do for me. I have to have answers that are clear and make sense. I won't take your answer if it's any nonsense like that.

SOCRATES. Thrasymachus, don't be hard on us. Polemarchus and I may have gone a little wrong in the argument, but it wasn't on purpose. Why, if we were only looking for gold, we wouldn't go about giving up points to one another and giving up with them all our chances of getting at the gold. But justice is something of much more value than gold. What makes you say that we are feebly giving way to one another and not doing our very best? (337) No, my good friend, that's not what you think. You see that the question is too hard for us. We aren't able enough. That's the secret. And if so, would it not be better for you and able men like you to have a little feeling for us instead of getting angry?

THRASYMACHUS. Hoo! Ha! How like Socrates! Always in the dark, aren't you? Always without any knowledge of what you are talking about! Didn't I see how it would be? Didn't

I say that, whatever the question, he wouldn't give an answer but would go on turning and tricking us? He'd do anything in place of answering.

SOCRATES. You are a wise man, Thrasymachus, and so are very certain that if the question is 'What is twelve?' and you won't take 'two times six' or 'three times four' or 'four times three' for an answer, you won't get any answer. That sort of nonsense won't do for you, will it? And what *do* you want? Am I not to give one of these answers, even if it's the right one? Have I to say something different, something that isn't true? Was that your idea, or wasn't it? What then? What would you say to that?

THRASYMACHUS. Pooh! How very much the same the two things are!

SOCRATES. There is nothing against their being the same. However, even if they were not, if one of these answers seems the right one to the person questioned, won't he say so? Will he be stopped by you or me saying that he isn't to?

THRASYMACHUS. Is that then what you are going to say? Are you going to give one of those answers I said I wouldn't take as *your* answer?

SOCRATES. I wouldn't be surprised if I did, if, after going into it all, that seemed to me the right answer.

THRASYMACHUS. If I give you a better answer than yours, you will have to pay me for it.

SOCRATES. I will, when I have any money.

GLAUCON. I have some money, Thrasymachus. If that is the only trouble, go on with your argument. We will all put our hands in our pockets for Socrates.

THRASYMACHUS. In order that he may do what he does all the time, put his questions and then take our answers to bits?

SOCRATES. Why, my friend, how is anyone to give answers (338) if he has not got them, or if some great authority has said that his ideas—such as they are—won't do? No, it's much better and more natural for you, who have all this knowledge, to give it to us. Don't grudge us your wisdom, but let Glaucon and the rest of us have it.

THRASYMACHUS. Here you have Socrates' wisdom! No teaching others, only learning from them, and not even a word of thanks.

SOCRATES. It is true about my learning from others, Thrasymachus. But that I won't give anything, that's false. I give what I have. I haven't any money or knowledge, so I have only approval to give. And I give that freely to those who do well, as you will see when you make a start yourself. For I know that you are going to say something good.

THRASYMACHUS. Very well. Let me have your best attention. Here is my answer. Justice is nothing but the interest of the stronger man. It is nothing but what does the stronger man good. Now. Why don't you say I am right? Ah, I knew you would do anything but that!

SOCRATES. Not at all! I am only waiting to see what you have in mind. And that, at present, I do not see. You say that the interest of the stronger is just. What on earth, Thrasymachus, is the sense of that? It isn't, I take it, anything like this—that if Polydamas is stronger than we are, and if it is in his interest as an athlete to take only red meat at his meals, then taking only red meat at our meals will be the just thing for us to do?

THRASYMACHUS. That's bad of you, Socrates. You are twisting my words to damage my statement.

SOCRATES. No, no! I am only attempting to see what the words say. Do be a little clearer.

THRASYMACHUS. Haven't you heard that the forms of government in different countries are different—that some have one ruler with complete power, some have a group as the rulers, and some are ruled by everyone together?

SOCRATES. Certainly.

THRASYMACHUS. And in every country isn't it the ruling power, the government, which is stronger?

SOCRATES. Quite so.

THRASYMACHUS. Moreover, every form of government makes laws with a view to its own interest—and by doing that, aren't they making it very clear that what is for the rulers' interest is what is just for the ruled? Whoever breaks (339) the law gets a punishment as being unjust. That is what my statement said. The government is the stronger, and its interest makes each thing just or unjust. Everywhere justice is the same thing, the interest of the stronger.

SOCRATES. I see now what you are saying. Everywhere justice is the interest of the stronger, is it? But we have still to see if this is true or false. Be it noted you yourself, Thrasymachus, in your answer are saying that justice is interest or profit—the very thing I was specially not to do! However, in addition you say 'the interest of the stronger'.

THRASYMACHUS. A small addition, isn't it?

SOCRATES. It is not clear, so far, if it is small or great. But first we have to see if what you are saying is true. We will agree that justice is interest of some sort, but you go on to say 'of the stronger'. About this addition I am not so certain. Let us take a longer and nearer look.

THRASYMACHUS. Go on with your looking.

SOCRATES. I will. First, you do say that it is just for the ruled to keep the laws of the rulers?

THRASYMACHUS. I do.

SOCRATES. Are the rulers always right or do they sometimes make mistakes?

THRASYMACHUS. No doubt they sometimes do.

SOCRATES. Then, in making their laws, they may sometimes make them rightly, and sometimes not?

THRASYMACHUS. Probably.

SOCRATES. To make laws rightly is to make them so that they are in the ruler's interest or do good to the ruler? Isn't it? And to make them wrongly is to make them so that they don't do the ruler good? Is that so?

THRASYMACHUS. That is so.

SOCRATES. But the laws they make are to be kept by the ruled, aren't they? And to do so is just and right?

THRASYMACHUS. Yes.

SOCRATES. Then, by what you say, it's not only just and right to do what's in the interest of the stronger, but equally the opposite, what's not to his interest and does him damage.

THRASYMACHUS. What's that you're saying?

SOCRATES. What *you* say, it seems to me. Aren't we in agreement that the rulers in giving orders to the ruled are sometimes wrong about what is best for themselves? And that it's just and right for the ruled to do what the rulers have ordered? Aren't we in agreement on all that?

THRASYMACHUS. I take it we are.

SOCRATES. Then you'll have to take it that it is just and right to do what isn't for the good of the rulers, stronger though they be, whenever the rulers unknowingly give orders for what isn't in their interest.

O Thrasymachus, wisest of men, there is no way out from the fact that, in your view, the ruled have to do, as what is just, things which are not for the good of the stronger! Is that clear enough? (340)

POLEMARCHUS. Yes, by Zeus, Socrates. Nothing is clearer.

CLITOPHON. Yes, if it is your word which is to be taken.

POLEMARCHUS. There is no need to take anyone's word. Thrasymachus himself has agreed that the rulers may sometimes make laws which are not for their good, and that it is right and just for the ruled to keep them.

CLITOPHON. But in saying 'what is for the good of the stronger', he had in mind what seemed to them to be so. And this the ruled have to do, and it was this that he said is justice and right.

POLEMARCHUS. But that was not what he said.

SOCRATES. That is not important, Polemarchus. If Thrasymachus now says so, let us take him so. Now, Thrasymachus, was that your account of justice and right: that which seemed to the stronger to be to his interest?

THRASYMACHUS. Not in the least. Would I say that a man was the stronger at the very time when he was making his mistake?

SOCRATES. I certainly took you to be saying so when you said that the rulers sometimes make mistakes.

THRASYMACHUS. That is because you go in for tricks in your arguments, Socrates. Why, to take the nearest example, do you say that a medical man is being a good medical man at the very time that he goes wrong about a disease? Or that a man doing arithmetic is good at addition at the very time when he is going wrong in his addition? Or that a reasoner is strong in reasoning at the very time that he is giving the wrong reasons? We may say such things, but they are only a way of talking. For the fact is that an expert in any art never goes wrong in it so far as he is an expert. If he does go wrong, he is not being an expert in the art. In language rightly used, Socrates—and you are a great hand at talking about the right use of language—no expert is ever in error in so far as he is an expert. So no ruler goes wrong, in so far as he is a ruler. And so far as (341–2) he is a ruler, he gives orders for his own interest, for what is best for himself; and it is this that the ruled have to do. So, as I said at the start, what is just is what is best for the stronger.

SOCRATES. Good, Thrasymachus. My ways in argument seem to you full of tricks, do they?

THRASYMACHUS. They do!

SOCRATES. And you think I put those questions on purpose to damage your argument?

THRASYMACHUS. I've no doubt about that. But you will get nothing by it. You won't be able to make the least change in anything I say without my seeing through you. And you won't overpower me by open argument.

SOCRATES. My dear man, I won't attempt to. But to keep clear of this sort of thing in the future, do say clearly what you have in mind in talking of the ruler and the stronger man, as you have been doing. Is it the ruler in the general sense, or the ruler in the narrower sense, the expert in the art of ruling, the ruler in the truest sense?

THRASYMACHUS. It's the ruler in the truest possible sense of the word. And now do your worst. You won't get the better of me by your low tricks, and without tricks you are not strong enough to overcome me.

SOCRATES. I wouldn't attempt any such thing. I'm not out of my mind. Beard a lion! Trick Thrasymachus!

THRASYMACHUS. You were trying to, though it didn't come off!

SOCRATES. Enough of such talk. Let us hear a little more about this medical man, in the truest sense of the word 'medical'. Is he a helper of the sick or a money-maker?

THRASYMACHUS. A helper.

SOCRATES. So with everyone who has an art. Every art looks after its own interest. And its own interest is to be as much itself, and do its own work as well as it possibly can. And so its purpose is to do good to those on whom it is used, not to the expert in the art. The medical man, as a medical man, does good to those who are ill, not to himself—he only does himself good as an expert in that other art. So you see, Thrasymachus, the ruler, *as a ruler*, does good to those under his rule. As a ruler he keeps his eyes fixed on that purpose in all he says and does. And with that your account of justice is turned upside down, it seems to us all.

THRASYMACHUS. Socrates, have you got a nurse?

SOCRATES. What is this? Why don't you answer me instead of asking such a question?

THRASYMACHUS. Have (343) you no one to take care of you and wipe your nose for you when you need it? Why does she let you go about so without even knowing that sheep and their keepers are different?

SOCRATES. What makes you say that?

THRASYMACHUS. Your idea, it seems, is that the keepers of sheep have the good of the sheep in view; that they make them fat for the profit of the sheep and not for their own profit!

Are rulers of countries any different from keepers of sheep, and do they have any other thought, day or night, than what they will get out of them? You are so far out about the just and the unjust that you don't see that justice is simply what is to the stronger man's profit, and very much a loss to the weak people who let themselves be ruled; while injustice is the opposite and gets the upper hand over those who are so simple in every sense of the word—so simple and just. Being ruled, they do what is for his good who is stronger, and make him happy by being his servants. But they don't make themselves happy by being so just. Not at all! Take another look, my simple-minded Socrates. The just man comes out worst every time in his relations with the unjust. Look at any business. In any undertaking, did you ever see the just man get anything but the worst of it in the end? Or take their doings with the government, the income tax, say. Which of them gets off best? If he is in office, the just man is certain to have let his own business go to the dogs. He hasn't time for it, and he gets nothing out of it because he is just. And his friends before long will hate (344) him because he won't unjustly give them a leg-up. But with the unjust man, it's all the other way. And the most unjust man is the one who has the power to keep pocketing things on the greatest scale. The best way to see all this is by turning your eye on the highest and most complete form of injustice, the one which makes the man who does the wrong most happy and which makes the others who are wronged, and who wouldn't themselves do any such wrong, most unhappy. And that is tyranny—the rule of one man who by tricks and force puts everyone under him and takes away all they have, the highest things and the everyday things, public things and private things, not bit by bit but all together. For any one little bit of such wrongdoing he'd get a sharp punishment and the worst of names. When a man does such things on a small scale, he's a robber, a murderer, a kidnapper, a swindler, or a thief. But when a man, after taking away everything that his countrymen have, takes their bodies and minds as well and makes them his slaves, in place of all these hard names, he is called 'happy' and 'blessed', not only by his countrymen but by strangers and by all who are told the great story of how he was as unjust as it is possible to be. For it is not fearing to do injustice, but fearing that they will undergo it, which makes men give it hard names. And so, Socrates, injustice, as you see, is a stronger and a freer and a greater thing than justice. As I said at first, justice is what does good to the stronger, and injustice is what does good to oneself. Well, it's time I was off.

SOCRATES. What! Are you going now, Thrasymachus, after emptying this bucket of words over our heads like a bath? Will you go before you make us see, or let us make you see, if this is so or not? Is this a small question you are answering, or is it about nothing less than our whole way of living by which each of us may get the best out of life?

THRASYMACHUS. Have I said that it isn't?

SOCRATES. It would seem, though, you don't care (345–6) much about us, or if we go on living better or worse without this knowledge you say you have. For my part, you haven't changed my view. I still do not see that the unjustest man gets more from being unjust than the just man gets from being just. Maybe there are others too who are still of this same opinion. So do make it clear that we are not in the right when we put justice higher than injustice.

THRASYMACHUS. What can I do? If what I've said won't make you see it, what will? Must I hammer it into your heads?

SOCRATES. Don't do that! There's no need to. But, in the first place, when you have said a thing, keep to it, and don't be all the time changing its sense. Or if you make a change, do so openly. As it is, you see, Thrasymachus—to go back to the earlier example—you made a start by taking the medical man in the narrow sense, the truest sense of the word, but you didn't do that when you came to the man who keeps sheep. As a keeper of sheep, he takes care of the sheep for their good, though as a money-maker or a man who is going to make a meal of them, he does so for his own good. Every form of art or rule, public or private, cares for what is under it, not for its own profit. You didn't get out of that by what you said. No one willingly takes other men's troubles in hand without some reward. Why, the very rulers need payment for ruling, which is a clear (347) sign that their work as rulers is not for their own good. And the payment will be in money or position or in punishment for them if they will not.

GLAUCON. How is that, Socrates? I do not see how the punishment comes in.

SOCRATES. Then you don't know why the best men take office. It is a bad thing to desire money or position in and for itself, isn't it?

GLAUCON. It is.

SOCRATES. That's why the good are not willing to rule for money or position, and why it's thought to be shameful to attempt to get into office oneself and not wait to be put there. But the chief punishment for not taking office is to be under the rule of someone worse than oneself. And this is the reason, it seems to me, why the better men take office. They do not go into it hoping to get any pleasure or profit from it. They take it as a necessary evil and because they are not able to hand it over to better men than themselves. In a society of good men there would be as much competition to keep out of office as there is now to get into it. But when you say that injustice is better than justice, that seems to me a more important (348) point. Let us take that up. Come, Thrasymachus, would you say that justice is a good thing and injustice a bad thing?

THRASYMACHUS. Is that probable, O simple Socrates, when I said that injustice gives a profit and justice gives a loss?

SOCRATES. What would you say then?

THRASYMACHUS. The opposite.

SOCRATES. What! Is being just a crime?

THRASYMACHUS. No, but it's being simple-minded or having an over-good heart.

SOCRATES. Then is being unjust having a *bad* heart?

THRASYMACHUS. No, it's having a good *head*.

SOCRATES. But do you see the unjust as being thoughtful and good?

THRASYMACHUS. Yes, if they are able to be unjust enough, able to overcome countries and armies. But maybe you think I am talking about pickpockets. That may give a profit, a small one, if no one sees it done. But such things are of no account in comparison with the great things I am talking about.

SOCRATES. I've no doubt that you know what you are saying. But I am surprised that you put injustice with wisdom and the good and justice under the opposite heading.

THRASYMACHUS. Well, I do so put them.

SOCRATES. That is a stranger position, my friend, than any you have taken before. And if you are going as far as that, it will be harder to answer you. For if your position were only that injustice gives you a profit, while you let us say that it was still a bad thing, there would be a chance for everyday arguments. But, as it is, you clearly are going (349) to say that injustice is great and good and wise and all the other things we say justice is.

THRASYMACHUS. This time, you are quite right.

SOCRATES. Well, I won't give up, so long as I feel that you believe what you say.

THRASYMACHUS. How is it different to you if I believe it or not?

SOCRATES. No. It's all the same, Thrasymachus. But one more question. In being just, does a man desire to get the better of another just man?

THRASYMACHUS. Certainly not. If he did, he wouldn't be so pleasingly simple.

SOCRATES. But what about his doings with the unjust man? Wouldn't it seem to him just to outdo the unjust man?

THRASYMACHUS. Yes, but he wouldn't be able to!

SOCRATES. That is not my question: It's only, would the just man, in being just, outdo another just man or only the unjust?

THRASYMACHUS. Only the unjust.

SOCRATES. But how about the unjust man? Will he attempt to overcome the other unjust ones and the just ones as well?

THRASYMACHUS. Certainly, because he overcomes everybody.

SOCRATES. Good. Now let's have a look at some other examples. How about that expert medical man? In his care of us is he attempting to outdo other expert medical men?

THRASYMACHUS. No.

SOCRATES. Or take two men with an equal knowledge of music. Does one attempt to outdo the other in tuning his instrument?

THRASYMACHUS. No.

SOCRATES. But he would outdo a man with no knowledge (350) of music. Well, with all forms of knowledge or art and their opposites, one who knows does not outdo others who know, but only those who don't. Isn't that so?

THRASYMACHUS. It may be so, in such simple examples.

SOCRATES. But what about the ignorant man? Won't he attempt to outdo both those who know and those who don't?

THRASYMACHUS. He may.

SOCRATES. But the man who knows is wise.

THRASYMACHUS. Yes.

SOCRATES. Then those who know will outdo only those who don't know.

THRASYMACHUS. It would seem so.

SOCRATES. But foolish people will make attempts to outdo everyone. So the unjust are bad and foolish and the just are good and wise. Ha? I know it is a hot day, but why are you getting so red in the face, Thrasymachus? I've never seen that before.

But you were saying, Thrasymachus, that injustice is stronger than justice, weren't you?

THRASYMACHUS. Yes, but I don't agree and I have an answer. But, if I were to give it, you would say that I was going on talking forever. So let me have my say out, or if you have to put your questions, go on, and I'll simply say, 'Very good', from time to time, as we do to the old women in the middle of *their* stories.

SOCRATES. Not against your own beliefs.

THRASYMACHUS. Yes, if it will make you happy, Socrates.

SOCRATES. All right. I will go on putting the questions (351) and you may do what you will. If being just is being wise, it is not hard to see that justice is stronger than injustice. But what I am after is not quite so simple as that. Let's take a country, Thrasymachus. You would say that a country may attempt to overcome other countries unjustly?

THRASYMACHUS. Certainly, and that is what the best countries chiefly do, those whose injustice is most complete.

SOCRATES. Yes, but will the country which does this have the power to do so, if it's quite without justice, or will it only have such power through whatever justice is in it?

THRASYMACHUS. If what you were saying is right, that being just is being wise, it will be through justice; but if it's as I said, it will be through injustice.

SOCRATES. Very good, Thrasymachus. You not only say 'Yes' and 'No' but give the right answers.

THRASYMACHUS. I'm doing my best to please you, Socrates.

SOCRATES. It's very good of you. But one thing more. Will a country, or an army, or even a band of cut-throats attempting to work together get on well by wronging one another?

THRASYMACHUS. Certainly not.

SOCRATES. Fighting and hate and attempts to do one another down are the outcome of injustice. But from justice come love and harmony of mind. Is it not so?

THRASYMACHUS. So be it, not to be of a different opinion from you.

SOCRATES. How sweet of you, my friend. But take the (352–3) one man by himself, will not the injustice within him make him unable to do anything rightly because he will be fighting with himself? Won't he be against himself as well as against the just?

THRASYMACHUS. Very well, if you will.

SOCRATES. But the gods are just too?

THRASYMACHUS. All right. Let us say that they are.

SOCRATES. Then the just will be dear to the gods but the unjust not.

THRASYMACHUS. Go on enjoying yourself. I'll say nothing against you. I don't want to give your friends pain.

SOCRATES. Very well then. But there is this to add. Wouldn't you say that a horse, for example, has its own special sort of work to do? And in fact it is so with everything—as seeing is the work of the eyes and hearing the work of the ears. And don't all things do their special work through having their own virtue and being truly themselves? If an eye is less than itself or has something wrong with it, will it see well? And the same with the others things. Isn't it so?

THRASYMACHUS. It seems safe to say that's so.

SOCRATES. And is it not the same with the soul? Will it ever do its work well if it isn't itself, if all is not well with it or if it is without its virtue? And won't a bad soul do things badly?

THRASYMACHUS. Necessarily.

SOCRATES. And the virtue of a soul is justice?

THRASYMACHUS. Yes.

SOCRATES. Well then, when a man is living rightly he is happy, and when he is not he is unhappy? So, Thrasymachus, (354) the just are happy and the unjust are not happy.

THRASYMACHUS. Let this round off your entertainment at the feast of Bendis.

SOCRATES. You gave me my feast, now that you are gentle and no longer angry; but I was not well entertained because I tried to eat too much. Before seeing what justice is, I went on to the other question, 'Is the just man happier than the unjust man?' So that for me the outcome of the present discussion is that I know nothing. For without true knowledge of what justice is, how may I say for certain if it is a good thing or not, or if those who have it are or are not truly happy?

BOOK II

GLAUCON. Socrates! Would you make us really believe that it is better to be just than unjust? If so, you are (357) not doing it. Tell me, are there not some things we love for themselves, not for any after-effects? For example, the pleasures that do no damage, where the only outcome is the joy itself. There is that sort, isn't there?

SOCRATES. Yes.

GLAUCON. And there is another sort, isn't there, the things we love for themselves *and* for their after-effects? Reason, for example, and seeing, and being healthy. Aren't these things welcomed for two reasons: for themselves *and* for their out comes?

SOCRATES. Yes.

GLAUCON. And then, isn't there the third form of good, which takes in gymnastics, and medical care, and business? These are useful and, though they give us trouble, we go in for them—not for themselves but for the rewards which come from them. Wouldn't you say so?

SOCRATES. Why, yes! But what of it?

GLAUCON. In which of these sorts do you put justice?

SOCRATES. In the most beautiful, in my opinion. Among (358) the things which are to be loved for themselves *and* for their effects as well, by any man who hopes to be happy.

GLAUCON. But the masses, Socrates, don't think so. They put being just with hard work, as one of the things to be done only for what is to be got out of it, rewards and a good name. To them justice in itself is something to keep away from, because it gives trouble.

SOCRATES. Yes, that seems so, and we have been hearing quite enough from Thrasymachus against justice on that account. But I, it seems, am not very good at learning such things.

GLAUCON. Come now, hear what I have to say and see what

you think of it. Thrasymachus seemed to me to give up too soon, as if he were a snake you were putting to sleep with your voice. But I'm not so ready to say 'Yes!' to all this. For me, you will have to say what justice and injustice are and what their power is in the soul. Let us keep right away from all talk about rewards. Let me put Thrasymachus' argument again. First let us see what men say justice is, and what it comes from. Secondly, why those who keep to it do so with regret, as something necessary but not good in itself. And thirdly, why they act so; when, as *they* say, the unjust man has a much happier existence than the just man. They say so, Socrates. But that is not my belief, far from it. But I *am* completely at a loss when Thrasymachus and a thousand others keep up such an outcry about it. I haven't ever heard a statement about all this of the sort I need. Something in praise of justice in and for itself. And you are the man to give us that. Now let me stretch every nerve to get together all I may on the side of the unjust life, and so give an example of the sort of thing I'm waiting to hear from you against injustice and in praise of justice. Is that all right with you?

SOCRATES. Very much so. For there is nothing a man of sense would care more to talk about again and again.

GLAUCON. Good. Then let us take the first point first, what they say justice is and what it comes from.

They say that by nature to do wrong is a good thing; to undergo wrong an evil thing; but that the evil of undergoing wrong is greater than the good of wrongdoing. So, when men have wronged and been wronged by one another, (359) and have the taste of the two in their mouths, those who are without the power to do wrong or to keep from being wronged make an agreement with one another to put an end to both. And this is the start, they say, of ordered society, of law-making, and of agreements between men. And to the orders of the laws they give the name justice. It is a middle condition between the best—which is to do wrong—and the worst—

which is to be wronged without having the power to give a blow back. Justice, they say, being this middle way between these two, is respected, not as a thing good in itself, but as a thing we keep up because we are not strong enough to be unjust. No one who had the necessary force and who was fully a man would ever make such an agreement with anyone to do no wrong and, in turn, not be wronged. He would be out of his mind if he did.

That, then, is what justice naturally is, Socrates, and that is how it comes into being, on this theory.

Now for the second point—that the just are just unwillingly and through being too weak to be unjust. We will see this best by looking at an example, in which the just and the unjust are made free to do whatever they will. Keep them in view a bit and see where their desires will take them. We will come on the just man in the very act of becoming unjust. Every living being naturally desires to have more than others, and is only turned to the idea of equal rights by force and by law. Take the story of Gyges. He, it is said, was a keeper of sheep under the ruler of Lydia. In the fields where he took his sheep one wet summer, after a shaking of the earth, a great hole opened. He went in, and saw strange things. Among them a horse of brass, hollow and with a door into it, and within this door the body of a giant with a gold ring on its hand, and this ring he took away. At the month's end the keepers of sheep came together to send their report to the ruler. At this meeting he had the ring on his finger, and, by chance, the stone was turned to the (360) inside of his hand. And they were talking of him as if he weren't there, for they were not able to see him. Then he tested the ring. When the stone was outside he was seen, but when it was inside, no one saw him. And he kept all this secret, and had himself sent to the ruler, and when he came there, he made love to the Queen. With her help he put the King to death and became the ruler himself.

Now, if there were two such rings, and one were given to

the just and the other to the unjust man, what would they do? No one is so adamantine-souled that he would go on being just and keep his hands off other men's things, if he were free to take whatever he desired, go into any store or house, get into any bed, put anyone to death, or let anyone out of prison as the idea came to him—in short be like a god among men. The just man would do quite as the unjust man does. They wouldn't be different in any way. And this makes it clear that no one is willingly just. They are only forced to be just. For every man, if he is able to do wrong, does wrong. For he sees that to do wrong will profit him more than to do right; and that's true, so they say. And if anyone, having the power we are talking about, didn't make use of it for his own profit, he would be thought a poor foolish person, though men might praise him openly for fear of being wronged. So much for this point.

But to come now to the decision between these two ways of living: We'll only make it rightly if we keep the most completely just man and the most completely unjust man quite separate in our minds. Like this: take nothing of his injustice from the unjust and nothing of his justice from the just, but let them be completely so in all they do. The unjust man must be an expert in being unjust, in seeing what is possible and what isn't, in doing the one and (361) letting the other go. So our unjust man will get away with everything. If he doesn't, he is a bad worker. For the highest injustice is to seem just without being so. The man who is best at being unjust will have the greatest name for justice. Give him the power, if his ill-doings come to light, to talk people round or to use force, if force is needed, and to use the help of his friends and his money to make everything seem different.

Now put by the side of that our picture of the just man, the simple and noble man, whose purpose, as Aeschylus puts it, is not to seem but to *be* just. There will have to be no seeming. For if he seems just, he will be honoured; and it will not be clear that he isn't after the honour. So we have to take from him everything but his justice. We have to make him the opposite of the unjust man in every way. Let him be the best of men, and let him be thought the worst. Then only will he have been put to the test, and then only will we see if he is able to make way in the teeth of a bad name and all its outcomes. And let him go on unchanged to death, seeming all through to be most unjust through being just. After taking the two men so to the limit, the one of injustice, the other of justice, we will be ready to judge which of them is the happier.

SOCRATES. My word! Glaucon. You are polishing up your two men, as if they were statues going in for a competition.

GLAUCON. I do my best, Socrates, because if they are as I say, it won't be hard then to see what sorts of existences are waiting for them. Don't take this as my account. It is the account of those who put injustice higher than justice. What they say is, that the just man, if this is his behaviour, (362) will be whipped, put in chains, have his arms and legs broken, and his eyes burned out with the iron and, at last, after undergoing every sort of ill, he will be nailed on the cross. That's how he will come to see that it is not being but seeming just which is to be desired. And, they say, it is simply true that to the unjust man —the man who keeps his eye on things as they are, and whose desire is to seem just, not to be so—come first, office and a place in the government because of his name for justice; then a wife from a family that can help him and openings for his children to marry into any family he pleases; and connections which will let him mix in any other business with whomsoever he will; and in all this, profit and pleasure for himself—all because he has no troubles and doubts about being unjust. And, moreover, they say, if he goes to law, he gets the better of it, and becomes rich and able to do good to his friends and to harm those against him. And his offerings to the gods will be on a great scale. He will be a better servant to the gods than the just man. So they say that it would not be surprising if the gods were kinder to him too. So much better, they say, Socrates, is the existence waiting for the unjust man than for the just—at the hands of gods and men.

ADEIMANTUS. Don't take it, Socrates, that this statement against justice is a bit complete!

SOCRATES. Why, Adeimantus, what more is there to be said?

ADEIMANTUS. The most important point of all, Socrates, has not even been touched on.

SOCRATES. Then, as the saying goes, 'Let brother help brother'. If Glaucon is short in his reasons, do you make it up. Though, for my part, what he has said is quite enough to down me and take from me all power of helping justice.

ADEIMANTUS. You are not serious, Socrates. But let me say my say about the reasons and the language of those who praise justice. That will make what Glaucon has in mind clearer. Let us see how fathers and schoolteachers and all the others who are responsible for the young go on. They keep preaching all the time about the honour (363–5) that being just will get us, and about all the good things Glaucon has been saying come from a good name. And they put in as well all the rewards which the gods, they say, give to those who do right—in this existence and after it—and the punishments given to the unjust. And they have nothing more to say about justice.

And take account, Socrates, of the language that poets and others are always using about all this. About how being temperate and honest is all very fine and much to be honoured, of course, but it's unpleasant and hard work. And how having 'a good time', and not minding how you get it, is easy and only something people *say* they are against. They have always a good word for bad men who are rich or powerful enough and little or nothing to say to help anyone who is poor or in any way in need of help—though they will agree, easily enough, that the poor may be much better people than the rich and powerful. But the strangest thing of all, Socrates, is what is said about the gods: how the gods themselves send people good and evil—to good men evil and to bad men good. And there are priests and go-betweens who come to rich men's houses and make them believe that with prayers and offerings they have built up a great store of 'pull' with the gods, so that they can take care of any *trouble* the rich man or his forefathers may have got into with the gods. A feast, not at all a bad thing to be at, will do what is needed, they say. And if a man has an enemy he wants to harm, for a small payment they will help him to harm anyone he pleases, just or unjust. They have words and prayers that can make the gods themselves do what they say. And on all this they have the poets on their side. For example, Homer:

> The gods themselves are moved by prayers
> And men, by offerings and sweet-sounding words
> And incense and wine-droppings, turn their minds
> By prayers, when they have done evil and injustice.
>
> (*Iliad* IX, 499–501)

And they have any number of other poems which they use in their services, and they make not only people but rulers too believe that injustices can be made all right again through pleasant feasts and sport for the living. And as for the dead, they say that there are services and offerings which can save wrongdoers from evil outcomes of their wrongdoings. But those who will not pay for these services and offerings may get ready for the worst.

What, Socrates, will be the effect of all this on the souls of able young men, quick to fly from one opinion to another about how to go through life as happily as possible? Won't they say to themselves: 'The outcome of being just—if I don't seem just too—will be every sort of loss. But if while I'm being unjust I seem straight enough, I'll have a godlike time! Let me put on a front of justice; inside that, see to it that I get my profit. It may be hard to keep all secret, but every great thing is hard. And with a view to being secret, let us go in for the organization of secret societies and political clubs, and there are teachers of public speaking who are a help with meetings and with the law. That is the way to get on. And as for the gods, maybe there are none, or maybe they don't give any attention to our doings, so what is the point of trying to keep out of their (366) view? If there are gods and they are watching, well, the poets say that offerings have a great effect. Let us first get something to give them and all will then be well.'

After all this, Socrates, what chance is there that any young man who has great powers of mind or body, or money, or family, won't be ready to laugh to himself on hearing justice talked up?

Anyone who really knows that justice is best is very ready to understand the unjust. For he knows that only a few people—by something godlike in them—can keep clear of injustice and that for the others it is fear or feebleness of spirit or old age that makes them be against injustice. They are not strong enough to be unjust. All this is clear. As soon as one of these gets enough power he becomes as unjust as he can be.

The reason why I am saying all this is the fact which was the starting-point of our two speeches for Glaucon here and myself. The strange fact that you, Socrates, and all you self-named lovers of justice—from the great men of old times to the present day—don't ever say anything against injustice itself or for justice itself, but only go on about the good name and other rewards that come from them. But what the one or the other is in itself, when it's in the mind of its owner, out of the eyes of the gods or of other men, no one has ever made clear; or how injustice is the greatest of all evils which the mind may have within itself while justice is the greatest good. If you had (367) all said what they are from the very start, and from our earliest years up, and had made us see it, we wouldn't now be having to guard ourselves against one another's injustices. Everyone would be his own best guard, for fear that by working injustice he would be letting the worst evil into his mind and having to live with it there.

This, Socrates, is what I would have you give us. Make clear to us not only that justice is better than injustice, but what they are in themselves, and what makes them what they are. And put aside any ideas about the good or ill names they have, so that we don't take you to be talking about the seeming justice but only about the thing itself. All of your existence has been given up to thought about this. So don't any longer say the sorts of things which others may say, but make us see clearly what justice and injustice do to their owners, and why the one is good and the other bad.

SOCRATES. Well was it said of you, Glaucon and Adeimantus, (368) sons of the man we know, when you did such great things in the fighting at Megara: 'Sons of Ariston, of a line coming from a godlike father', for you must have a touch of the god-like to believe in justice, though you are able to say all this on the other side. I think you do believe in it because I know you. From your words by themselves I might have doubted it. But what can I say?

How am I to make what is true clear to you? You were not moved by the arguments I used against Thrasymachus. But I would be false to you and to the gods not to come to the help of justice when it is attacked, or not to say what I may while breath and voice are with me.

GLAUCON. Come to our help, Socrates. The need is great. Don't drop the argument till we come to the end, and the innermost being of justice is clear.

SOCRATES. For this question we need sharp eyes. How will it be, because we are not very able persons, to do as though we were reading small letters at a distance? If someone said that the same letters, but much greater, were to be seen in a different place, wouldn't that be a godsend? Wouldn't we take a look first at those great letters and then at the smaller to see if they are the same?

ADEIMANTUS. Yes, but where is the parallel?

SOCRATES. It is like this. There are two justices. There is the justice which is in one man, isn't there? And the justice which is in a country or society taken all together as one?

ADEIMANTUS. Certainly.

SOCRATES. Isn't the society greater than the man?

ADEIMANTUS. It is.

SOCRATES. Then, maybe, there would be more justice in (369) the greater thing. Or at least it may be less hard to see. Let us look for this quality in a state and only then go to the one man by himself, going from the greater to the less, looking for what is like the greater in the idea of the less.

ADEIMANTUS. A good suggestion.

SOCRATES. If we watched in thought how a society came into being, we would be watching the growth of justice in it.

ADEIMANTUS. Maybe.

SOCRATES. And if this were done, wouldn't there be more hope that what we are looking for would be seen with less trouble? Still, it is not a light bit of work. Take thought, are we to go through with it?

ADEIMANTUS. We have taken thought. Go on, Socrates, there is no turning back.

SOCRATES. At the start, a city or state, in my opinion, comes into being because no one of us is enough in himself. Every man is dependent on other men. Would you say there is any other cause for the growth of the first societies of men?

ADEIMANTUS. No, I'm in agreement with you.

SOCRATES. So, as we have a number of different needs, a number of different men come together in a common living place, one helping the others in one way, another in another, and this group of men is a society.

ADEIMANTUS. True.

SOCRATES. And between one man and another there is an

exchange of help, because every man takes this way of doing things to be better for himself.

ADEIMANTUS. Certainly.

SOCRATES. Come then, let us invent a state, but its maker in fact will be our needs.

ADEIMANTUS. Clearly.

SOCRATES. The first of our needs is food, the thing most necessary for life.

ADEIMANTUS. Yes.

SOCRATES. And our second need is housing and the third clothing and that sort of thing?

ADEIMANTUS. That is so.

SOCRATES. How large will our society have to be to give us all these things? Won't we have to have a farmer and a builder and a maker of clothes? And how about a shoemaker, and some other workers to take care of the needs of the body?

ADEIMANTUS. Right.

SOCRATES. Then the very least number of men enough for such a society would be four or five.

ADEIMANTUS. It seems so.

SOCRATES. Will every one of them work for the needs of all? Will the farmer, for example, by working four times as long, produce four times as much food as would be (370) enough for himself and divide it between them? Or will he do nothing for the others, but only produce enough food for himself in a quarter of the time and give the rest of his time to building, making clothes and shoes for himself, and so on?

ADEIMANTUS. Maybe, Socrates, the first way would be better.

SOCRATES. I wouldn't be surprised if it were. But it comes into my mind, Adeimantus, now that you say this, that we are not all the same in our powers. One man is good at one thing, another at another. Isn't that so?

ADEIMANTUS. It is.

SOCRATES. So more things are produced, and better things,

when every man does what he can do best, without being troubled by having to do other things in addition.

ADEIMANTUS. Yes, certainly.

SOCRATES. Then, there will be a need for other workers. For someone to make the farmer's plough for him and so on.

ADEIMANTUS. True.

SOCRATES. But if so, our society will be very quickly increased.

ADEIMANTUS. Certainly.

SOCRATES. Still, it wouldn't be very great even if we put in men to keep sheep and added oxen for the farmer's ploughing and for transport and for skins and so on.

ADEIMANTUS. It wouldn't be very small if it had all that.

SOCRATES. But it is almost impossible to put our society in a place where it wouldn't need things that have to come from other countries.

ADEIMANTUS. It is.

SOCRATES. So we will have to have traders, and the traders (371) will in addition have to have things to give in exchange for the goods they get. So we will have to have more farmers and other workers. And if the trade goes overseas, we will have to have sailors.

ADEIMANTUS. Quite a number!

SOCRATES. But how about the division of all these common goods which was the purpose of the society from the start?

ADEIMANTUS. We'll have to have a market.

SOCRATES. Yes, and money as a sign for the purpose of exchange. That will be the outcome of all this?

ADEIMANTUS. No question.

SOCRATES. When the farmer takes his produce to the market and gets there before anyone comes who desires it, is he to be seated there doing nothing? What about his loss of working hours?

ADEIMANTUS. But there are men who see to this need; in well-ordered towns they are generally those who are feeble in body and no good for any other work.

SOCRATES. Those are the storekeepers, but the traders go from town to town.

ADEIMANTUS. Certainly.

SOCRATES. And, moreover, aren't there other servants of the society, who, maybe, in things of the mind are not quite up to the level of the rest, but their bodies are strong? And they sell their work for a price. Well then, Adeimantus, is our society now complete?

ADEIMANTUS. Maybe.

SOCRATES. Now where, in this society, will we see justice and injustice? In which of these parts which we have put in?

ADEIMANTUS. I don't see them, Socrates, if they are not (372) in some need which those very parts have for one another.

SOCRATES. That may be a good suggestion, Adeimantus. We will go into it farther. And let us first see what sort of existence the men and women in this society will have. They will make bread and wine and clothes and shoes. They will be builders of houses. And in summer they will do their work for the most part without clothes or shoes, but will put them on in winter; won't it be so? And for food, they will have meal from their grain and make cakes from it on clean leaves or something of that sort, stretching themselves out on simple beds covered with flowers. They will be happy with their young sons and daughters, drinking their wine with more flowers in their hair and making up songs to the gods. A happy company, not producing more than enough offspring for fear of getting into need or war.

GLAUCON. But with nothing to give a taste to their food!

SOCRATES. True, I was overlooking that. Well, let them have salt, olives, and cheese, and onions and greens, and the sorts of things they boil in a pot in the country, and nuts and berries. With such healthy meals, and keeping within measure in their drink, long may they go on living at peace, and hand on, at the end, the same existence to their offspring after them.

GLAUCON. Yes, Socrates, and if you were forming a society for pigs, what other food would you supply?

SOCRATES. But what would you have, Glaucon?

GLAUCON. Why, give them the common things which are now in use. Seats, tables to have their meals on, and meats and sweets such as we now have, if they are not to be very poor and unhappy.

SOCRATES. So be it. I see your point. We are watching the growth of a society which does itself well. Very good. Maybe that is not such a bad suggestion. In such a society we may see better where justice and injustice come in. The true society, in my view, is the one we have been watching—the healthy society, as it were. But if it is (373) your pleasure that we take a look at a fevered society, I have nothing against it. For there are some, it seems, for whom this sort of existence with this sort of food is not enough. They have to have all the apparatus of the present day, players and dancers and song girls, and all these of every sort; and if we go beyond the necessary things I was talking of, we'll have to put into our society all the arts of the painter and the threadworker, and all their materials, and have gold and silver and the rest as ornaments.

GLAUCON. True.

SOCRATES. Then, we'll have to make our limits much wider. The first healthy society is not enough. There will have to be great numbers of workers in the arts, painters and poets and musicians and instrument-makers, and makers of all sorts of things—specially those who make women's dresses. And even servants. Won't teachers be needed, and nurses, wet and dry, men and women hairdressers, and sweetmeat-makers and cooks, as well as pig-keepers, who had no place in the earlier society? And there will be other sorts of animals, if we have a taste for that sort of food.

GLAUCON. All that, certainly.

SOCRATES. And living in this way, we will have more need for medical men than before, won't we?

GLAUCON. Much more.

SOCRATES. And the country which was enough for the support of the first group will not be great enough now?

GLAUCON. True.

SOCRATES. Then a bit of some other group's land will be needed by us for our farmers, and they will need a bit of ours if they, like ourselves, have gone beyond the limits of the necessary and given themselves up to getting things without end.

GLAUCON. It has to be so, Socrates.

SOCRATES. Then we will go to war, Glaucon. That's the step which comes now. Isn't it?

GLAUCON. Even so.

SOCRATES. Well, we will not now go into the bad and the good sides of war; but will only say this. Here we see the starting-point of war. It comes to states from the very things from which the worst evils, public and private, come to us.

GLAUCON. Undoubtedly.

SOCRATES. Then our society has to be greater still. And (374) this time the addition is nothing less than a complete army! Ready to go out fighting for all that they have *now* as well as for what we were talking about.

GLAUCON. Why, aren't they strong enough to do that themselves?

SOCRATES. No. Not if we were right in saying that one man won't be good at a number of different arts. Is not war an art? And an art needing as much attention as shoemaking?

GLAUCON. True.

SOCRATES. So we will have to take great care to get men (375) with the right natural qualities for this, the most important sort of work: guarding the state/They will have to be like good watchdogs: quick to see who is against them, strong fighters, and free from fear. That is, they must be spirited. How great a thing spirit is; whoever has it fears nothing and is never overcome. So the first thing in a guard is to be spirited.

GLAUCON. Yes.

SOCRATES. But then how will we keep them from being violent with one another and the rest of the society?

GLAUCON. That is hard to get round.

SOCRATES. These fighting men have to be gentle to their friends, and a danger only to their enemies. If not, they won't wait till destruction comes to their people from the other side, but will be that destruction themselves.

GLAUCON. True.

SOCRATES. What are we to do, then? Where are there souls which are gentle and high-spirited at once? No one who is not both can possibly make a good guard. If these are opposites, as it seems, then a good guard is an impossible thing.

GLAUCON. So it seems, Socrates.

SOCRATES. Well may we be at a loss, my friend! We haven't kept our example in view—the well-trained watchdog who is gentle to his friends but the opposite to strangers! And isn't there a suggestion here that a good guard will have to be a lover of knowledge? A 'philosopher'?

GLAUCON. How so? I don't see that!

SOCRATES. Don't these dogs, when they meet a stranger, (376) become angry *before* he has done anything against them; but when they see an old friend, they give him a welcome, though they may never have got any good from his hands? Isn't that a sign of a true love of knowledge in a dog? The only thing separating friend from enemy for him is that he knows the one and doesn't know the other! So may we not say of a man as well, that if he is to be gentle to his friends and family and relations, he will have to have a turn for philosophy?

GLAUCON. Be it so!

SOCRATES. Then, the good guard for our society will be a lover of learning (a philosopher, that is), high-spirited, quick in his acts, and strong. And now, by what education may we best make such men? Do you think to look into this will help us to see what justice is?

ADEIMANTUS. I think it will help very much.

SOCRATES. Now what should this education be? We will hardly get anything better than that which has already been well tested by experience in the past. That is, gymnastics for the body and music for the soul. And we will start, will we not, with music—not with gymnastics?

ADEIMANTUS. We will.

SOCRATES. Under music don't we put stories, true and (377) false, and don't we start with the false stories first?

ADEIMANTUS. How's that?

SOCRATES. Aren't the first stories we give the young generally false, though there may be something true in them? And in every work, are not the first steps the most important, above all with soft young minds, for then the form one is attempting to give them is most readily taken?

ADEIMANTUS. Very true.

SOCRATES. So will we let these young things go on hearing any stories anyone may make up, and get into their minds ideas generally the very opposite of those it would be best for them to have when they come to their full growth as men?

ADEIMANTUS. No, don't let us do that on any account.

SOCRATES. Then we will keep a sharp eye on these makers of stories. But we will have to do away with most of the stories that are in use today, and chiefly those great false stories that Hesiod and Homer have been telling us.

ADEIMANTUS. How about some examples?

SOCRATES. Why, take the stories of the first gods, of (378) Uranos and Cronos and his sons. If those were the true facts, would it be right to give them to young and inexperienced persons without keeping anything back? No, if I had my way, I'd keep them quite secret. Or, if they had to be handed on, let them be given to as small a number of hearers as possible, and then only after the offering not of a pig but of something of so much value that it would keep the number down.

ADEIMANTUS. Certainly, they are hard to accept.

SOCRATES. They are. Let us have no more of them, or of any stories about gods and heroes fighting with one another. For if the gods are pictured so, men will say 'We may as well be as they are'. Our guards are to see it as a most shameful thing ever to war against one another. So let us keep out all these stories, for a young mind does not see how stories which are only parallels or comparisons are not the same as stories which are true in fact. And whatever is taken into the mind when it is young has a tendency to become fixed. So let us see that the first stories they hear be those which say most beautifully what the true values are.

ADEIMANTUS. There is reason in that. But if anyone says, 'Which stories are these?' what will our answer be?

SOCRATES. Why, Adeimantus, you and I are not poets, at present, (379) but builders of a society. The builders will say what the fictions have to do, but they are not forced to make up the stories themselves.

ADEIMANTUS. You are right. But of the gods what is to be said?

SOCRATES. In general, may we say this? It is right, I take it, in all ways to give to God the qualities he truly has whatever sort of verses we may be making?

ADEIMANTUS. Yes.

SOCRATES. Then is not God certainly good, truly good, and always to be pictured so?

ADEIMANTUS. Without question.

SOCRATES. Well, but nothing which is good does damage or ill, does it?

ADEIMANTUS. No.

SOCRATES. Then that which is good is not the cause of all things, but only of things which are as it is right for them to be. So that which is good is not responsible for the coming into being of evil.

ADEIMANTUS. Right.

SOCRATES. If that be so, then God, inasmuch as he is good, is not the cause of all things, as the common belief goes. No, from him comes only a small part of the events of man's existence; the greater part does not come from him. For our evils are far greater in number than our goods. And though the good things come from no other than God, the causes of the ill things are in something other, not in him.

ADEIMANTUS. That seems to me most true.

SOCRATES. Then away with all the sayings in Homer (380) that God gives good *and* evil chances (*Iliad* XXIV, 527) or that the fact that agreements between men are broken came from God (*Iliad* II, 69) or that God sends diseases on families or destruction on countries—as with Troy. We will not let anyone say this sort of thing. Or if he does he will have to put in a theory, as well, that what God has done is right and good, and that the punishment is for the good of those who undergo it. We won't let it be said that anything which made men worse came from God. No. No fiction saying that God, who is good, is the cause of evil to anyone may be given out in our society, if it is to be a well-ruled society. Such language is damaging and in fact goes against its very self.

ADEIMANTUS. I am for this law, and well pleased with it.

SOCRATES. This then is one of the laws of the state, which poets will have to keep, that God is not the cause of all things, but only of the good. And here is a second law for you. Will God seem at any time or in any place to be different from himself? Will he come before men in all sorts of strange and different forms?

ADEIMANTUS. I don't see the answer, right away.

SOCRATES. If anything is changed from its true form, won't the change have to be produced by itself or by some other thing?

ADEIMANTUS. Yes.

SOCRATES. And don't the best things undergo the least changes and motions that come to them from *other* things? For example, the body is changed by meat and drink and work, and every plant by the light of the sun and the wind and such things. But isn't the change least in the plant or body that is healthiest and strongest?

ADEIMANTUS. Undoubtedly it is.

SOCRATES. So of the soul. It will be the most fearless and (381) thoughtful soul which is least moved and changed from without. That is so of things which have been made by men: houses, clothes, and so on; those that are well made and in good condition will be least changed by time and other forces.

ADEIMANTUS. True.

SOCRATES. So that whatever is naturally good or well made by art will be least able to be changed from without?

ADEIMANTUS. So it would seem.

SOCRATES. But certainly God and the things that are his are in every way best. So it is very improbable that he will be changed into different forms *from without*.

ADEIMANTUS. Very improbable.

SOCRATES. But will he be changed by himself?

ADEIMANTUS. If he is changed at all.

SOCRATES. By changing, would he make himself worse or better? More or less beautiful?

ADEIMANTUS. Worse, necessarily, if he is changed at all, for we are taking it that nothing is better or more beautiful than God.

SOCRATES. Quite so. And will any god or any man consciously make himself worse than he is? So, Adeimantus, God, inasmuch as he is as beautiful and good as possible, will not change himself. He will keep, simple and unchanging, his right form, forever. So let no poets tell us that the gods go about among men in all sorts of disguises.

But maybe, Adeimantus, though the gods are unchanging, they make us think that they put on different forms. What is your view?

ADEIMANTUS. I'm not certain.

SOCRATES. Would a god be ready to be false, as you see (382) it, by putting false seemings before our eyes? Are you not certain that things which are 'truly false', if I may put these words together so, are hated by all gods and all men?

ADEIMANTUS. I don't see that.

SOCRATES. False beliefs in the chief part of oneself, and about the chief things, are what no one consciously lets himself have. No! More than anything, everyone is in fear of false beliefs there.

ADEIMANTUS. I still do not see it.

SOCRATES. Because you take me to have some very deep idea. But it is simply this. To have false beliefs in one's own soul and so to be without true knowledge about how things are as they are—that is the last thing to which any man agrees. For all men especially hate to be wrong about things like that.

ADEIMANTUS. Yes, that is specially hated

SOCRATES. This is what being 'truly false' is: when the soul does not know that it's going wrong in its very self. The false statement someone makes, the false word, is a sort of copy or picture of the earlier form in the mind and not itself an unmixed error. Or am I wrong?

ADEIMANTUS. No, you are quite right.

SOCRATES. Then anything truly false is hated, not by the gods only but by all men?

ADEIMANTUS. Yes.

SOCRATES. But sometimes aren't false statements of use to us? And are they rightly hated then? But when are they of use to us? Isn't it when we are keeping off our enemies? Or when our friends are attempting to do something foolish, or are out of their minds? Isn't it then that a false statement may be a good thing, like a medicine, as a way of turning them from their purpose? And in those stories of the gods we were talking about, isn't it our ignorance of the true history of the earliest times which makes them of use to us—the false is made as like as may be to the true?

ADEIMANTUS. That is right.

SOCRATES. But how will false statements be of use to God?

Not for this last reason, for he has the knowledge. There is no false poet in God. And will he be false through fear of his enemies?

ADEIMANTUS. Far from it.

SOCRATES. Or because his friends are foolish or out of their minds?

ADEIMANTUS. No, no one of this sort can be a friend of God.

SOCRATES. God is a completely simple and true being, in word and in act, unchanging in himself and sending no (383) seemings to others, when they are awake or in sleep.

ADEIMANTUS. I believe so, Socrates, as you say it.

SOCRATES. So, as our second law for what may be said about the gods: they do not change their forms or send false seemings to us in words or acts. Though we may love and honour Homer and Aeschylus and other poets we will not let them tell children that the gods do any such things. We will be angry with anyone who says they do; and we will not let teachers use him in the education of the young, if our guards are to be god-fearing men and godlike as far as men may be.

ADEIMANTUS. Certainly, let these be our laws.

BOOK III

SOCRATES. Such then will be our teaching about the gods, if the young are to honour them and their own fathers and mothers. (386–8) And if we would have our guards be brave, will we not keep from them all stories about what comes after death which might make them fear it?

ADEIMANTUS. We will.

SOCRATES. And we will ask Homer and the other poets not to be angry if we cut out of their works all verses in which Hades and the after-life are pictured as fearful or hateful. And this not because such things are unpoetic, but because the more poetic they are the more they may make people afraid of death.

ADEIMANTUS. It is so.

SOCRATES. Away then with all the sad outcries against death! We say that a good man will not see death as a bad thing for another good man, his friend, to undergo.

ADEIMANTUS. We will say so.

SOCRATES. Such a man has within himself, in the highest degree, whatever is necessary for a happy existence, and he, of all things on earth, is least dependent on other things. So by him, less than by anyone, is the loss of a son or a brother, or even of all that he has, to be feared. So less than any will he cry out in pain when the loss comes.

ADEIMANTUS. Less than any.

SOCRATES. So away with all the songs into which those feelings of loss are put. And we will ask Homer and the other poets again not to show us Achilles, the son of a goddess, rolling from side to side, now on his back, now on his face, in his grief (*Iliad* XXIV, 10), or as putting handfuls of black, burnt-out ashes on his head, or as keeping up all that sorrowing that Homer makes so much of. And even less should he represent the gods as grieving over Hector (*Iliad* XXII, 168) or Sarpedon (*Iliad* XVI, 433). For, my dear Adeimantus, if our young people listen seriously to such things, instead of laughing at them, how are they to develop self-control? And on the other hand, our guards are not to be much given to violent laughing, for after that generally comes an equally violent reaction.

ADEIMANTUS. To the best of my belief, it does.

SOCRATES. So we won't let Homer tell us about the gods laughing long to see Hephaestus pouring wine for them and so on. But again, and most of all, truth is to be prized. (389) For, if we were right in what we said just now, and false statements are of no use to the gods and only of use to men as a sort of medicine, it is certain that such a power will have to be kept in the hands of medical men. Others may have no part in it.

ADEIMANTUS. Clearly.

SOCRATES. Only for the rulers of the state, if for any, will it be right to make use of false statements, in order to give false suggestions for the good of the state. No others may do so. It will be worse for a private person to be false to his rulers than for an ill man to tell lies to his doctor or a sailor to report falsely about the ship to his captain. So if the authorities see anyone in the society using false statements they will punish him for doing what will overturn a state as much as a ship.

ADEIMANTUS. They will if this state ever comes into being.

SOCRATES. And the young in our society will have to be self-controlled. That is: first, do what they are ordered to do by the authorities; secondly, *themselves* rule their desires as to food and drink and love-making. And with this in (390–4) view, we will again keep an eye on what they are reading and hearing all the time; and keep out every sort of story which will make it harder for the young to become self-controlled: things like Achilles saying to Agamemnon, 'You full wineskin, you with the face of a dog and the heart of a faun' (*Iliad* I, 225), or like Hera putting Zeus to sleep on topmost Gargarus (*Iliad* XIV, 294–341).

ADEIMANTUS. I am in full agreement.

SOCRATES. So much then for what is put into these stories, but the same will be true of how they are made, the form, the measure, the rhythm of the verses, and all the ways of representation which are used in them. All the harmonies and all the rhythms which may make men less true to themselves, less self-controlled, we will keep out. And specially on account of these guards of ours. And as to them, are they to be good at these arts of story-making and verse-writing, and acting? Didn't we say that the same persons are not able to do different things equally well?

ADEIMANTUS. Yes, and we were right to say so.

SOCRATES. Then our guards will not themselves go (395–400) deeply into other arts, so that they may become as good as it is possible for men to be at the all-important art which *is* their business—that of making and keeping their country free. And in the art of speaking, so far as that is their business, the rule will be the same with them as with all users of language. The rhythm and motion of the words are to come from the outlook of the mind; they are to be the natural rhythms of a well-controlled and manlike way of living.

ADEIMANTUS. Certainly.

SOCRATES. Good language and good harmony and rhythm are all dependent on a 'good nature' or 'good form'—not the sort of thing commonly named 'good nature' or 'good form', but a mind which is truly well made in its inner being.

ADEIMANTUS. Right.

SOCRATES. And isn't it necessary for the young to be influenced by these qualities everywhere, if they are to do what (401) is truly theirs to do? And these qualities may be seen in everything, in painting, and in ornament, in the making of everything, clothes, buildings, pots...and in the forms of living things. In all these, order or good form and its opposite have their places. Things without order, rhythm and harmony go with ill words and ill feelings, but good order goes with courage and self-control.

ADEIMANTUS. I see you are right.

SOCRATES. So, while keeping an eye on the poets and story writers in our society, won't we go farther and watch over the workers in all the other arts as well, and see that they do not put unshapely or ill-conditioned or ugly forms into their representations of living things, or into buildings or any other work of their hands? And let us keep those who are not able to do better from working in our society—so that our guards will not go on living and coming to their full growth among badly formed things, taking the evil in every day, as from unhealthy fields, little by little till, unconsciously, they have got a great mass of evil in their inmost souls. Wouldn't it be better to get workers of another stamp, with the natural power to see very clearly what is good and beautiful so that our young men and women, living, as it were, in a healthy country, would all the time be drinking in good from every side; so may it come upon their eye or ear like a sweet wind from a cleaner land and little by little from their earliest days make them like to, and friends with, and in harmony with the beautiful measure of reason?

GLAUCON. Such an education would be by far the best.

SOCRATES. That, Glaucon, is why music is so all-important in education. Because rhythm and harmony go down most deeply into the depths of the soul, and take the strongest grip upon it, and are able to give a man order if he is rightly trained in them. He that has been rightly trained will, moreover, have the sharpest eye for what is not beautiful, in works of art or in natural growths; and rightly turning away from them, will give his praise to what is beautiful, delighting in it and taking it into himself to become (402) noble and beautiful himself. But fixed will be his hate of all disgusting things, even when very young, before he is able to see the reason; and when reason comes, most warmly will he welcome her, being used to her through her connection with these earlier things and because he has had this education.

GLAUCON. No doubt this is why we have what we call 'music' in education.

SOCRATES. In learning to read we had to see the letters rightly, and respect them equally in a small word or in a great, taking care to keep them clear everywhere, believing we would be no experts till we did so.

GLAUCON. True.

SOCRATES. Could we know images of letters seen in still water or a looking glass before we knew the letters themselves? Are not these two knowledges parts of the same art?

GLAUCON. Indeed they are.

SOCRATES. Well, to go now from my example to the things of which it is an example. Will we ever become truly good at music ourselves—or will the guards we say we are teaching—before we have a knowledge of the true forms of self-control and courage and of being free-handed and great-minded? And all the other sister qualities, and their opposites as well, wherever they are? Must we not be able to see them clearly, themselves and their images, respecting them in all ways and in all places, in small things and in great, believing that the knowledge of these forms and of their images are parts of the same art?

GLAUCON. Yes, certainly this has to be so.

SOCRATES. Is our theory of music now complete? At all (403–9) events it has come to an end at the right place; for music, I take it, will best come to an end in the love of the beautiful.

So much for music. Now as to gymnastics. We need not go into detail. For in my opinion it is a good soul that makes the body as good as it can be—not the other way round.

GLAUCON. I think so too.

SOCRATES. So if we train the mind rightly we can hand over the care of the body to it. For example our guards must not over-drink. They have to know what they are doing and where they are.

GLAUCON. Yes. For a guard to need a guard would be laughable.

SOCRATES. And so too with over-eating. These guards are athletes in the greatest of all games, are they not?

GLAUCON. They are.

SOCRATES. Then ought they to eat as athletes eat?

GLAUCON. Maybe.

SOCRATES. No, athletes are too sleepy most of the time and they easily become ill. Our guards have to have the sharpest possible eyes and ears and be ready for every sort of living condition, keeping healthy through every change of weather. One might learn that much even from Homer. He does not feast his heroes on fish, though they are at the seaside on the Hellespont, nor on boiled meat, but only on roast. It is easier for soldiers just to use the fire than to take pots and pans about with them. And he says nothing anywhere about sweetmeats. People in good training know why.

GLAUCON. They do indeed.

SOCRATES. Those who attempt to do and have *everything* are like the music which mixes all measures. Keeping things simple makes for self-control in the soul and health in the body. And as bad behaviour and ill-health increase in a city so do doctors and law-courts. It is a sign that something is very wrong with it when free men take the art of medicine and law-court business so seriously.

GLAUCON. What can they do?

SOCRATES. Isn't it shameful and a mark of wrong education when a man takes to spending most of his time bringing charges against others before judges or defending himself from them—thinking himself very clever to be able to 'get by with' almost anything? How little sense of true values such a man has—not to know how much better it would be not to need jurymen ready to shut their eyes to such things! And as to illness, a life spent in the doctor's hands is no life at all for anyone with his work to do. And Asclepius himself knew this and knew better than to teach his followers—the Asclepiads or 'sons of Asclepius'—how to keep people living when they would be better dead. In his day what you did for the wounded or ill was simple. Homer, you remember, lets Diomede give the wounded Eurypylus (or was it Machaon?) wine with barley and cheese in it and has not a word to say against Patroclus for letting this be done.

GLAUCON. You have a great respect for Asclepius, I see.

SOCRATES. Yes, and rightly. And that is why I won't believe what the tragedians and Pindar say: that Asclepius, though he was Apollo's son, took a bribe of gold to save a man who was at the point of death and for that was struck by lightning. I won't believe either statement. If he was the son of a god he wouldn't take a bribe. And if he did take a bribe, he was not the son of a god.

GLAUCON. But you do think we ought to have good doctors and judges? And won't the best ones be those who have had most experience with all sorts and conditions of men?

SOCRATES. Of course, I want them good. But do you know which I would think good ones?

GLAUCON. I'll know if you will tell me.

SOCRATES. I'll try, but you have put two very different questions together.

GLAUCON. How?

SOCRATES. Doctors and judges are different. It is all right for a good doctor to have been ill in all sorts of ways himself. That may help him to understand diseases. Being ill need not have damaged his mind. But a mind that is or has been evil can't do anything rightly.

GLAUCON. True.

SOCRATES. A judge must not have been mixed up in wrong-doing himself. A good judge does not know evil from his own experience of it in himself, but from long years of training in understanding injustice as a strange thing that has somehow come into souls which are not themselves.

GLAUCON. That, at least, seems to be the most high-minded sort of judge.

SOCRATES. And a good one—which was the point of your question. Whoever has a good soul is good. The trickster who knows about evil from within often seems very clever when he is with people like himself. He is on his guard and keeps his eye on the patterns within him. But when he is among good people he seems stupid. He is uncertain how to take them. He has nothing in himself by which to measure them.

GLAUCON. I agree.

SOCRATES. So in our city we will have laws and an art of medicine of this sort:—to take care of the bodies and souls of those who are truly well made. But those who are not they will let die. And those who have in their souls evil which cannot be taken away, they will put to death.

GLAUCON. The best thing for them and for the state.

SOCRATES. So these will be the music and gymnastics that we need. Am I right, Glaucon, in saying that in making (410) up this system of education in music and gymnastics, our purpose is not, as some would say, to take care of the body with gymnastics and of the soul with music?

GLAUCON. What is it, if that is not so?

SOCRATES. Probably both are for the good of the soul.

GLAUCON. How so?

SOCRATES. In your experience, Glaucon, aren't those who have done gymnastics throughout, without doing music, rough and hard? And those who have only done the music, soft and feeble?

GLAUCON. O yes. The gymnastic ones are too rough and the others much softer than is good for them.

SOCRATES. But being rough comes from the spirited part, which if rightly trained will make a man free from fear, but if it's overdone, he probably will become hard and unpleasing.

GLAUCON. Right.

SOCRATES. And gentleness is produced by philosophy or the love of knowledge! If this is overdone he becomes soft, but when rightly guided, he is made gentle and well ordered.

GLAUCON. True.

SOCRATES. But we said that in our guards we must have these qualities united and in harmony. And where there is this harmony we will have minds which are both brave (411) and temperate. And without this harmony the mind is full of fear, and violent.

GLAUCON. Very much so.

SOCRATES. So, when a man gives himself up to music and lets his mind be breathed through by those sweet and soft and sad harmonies we were talking about, in such a man, at first whatever spirit he has is made soft and useful. At first: but if he goes on and gives way to these pleasures, then, little by little, his mind turns to liquid and wastes away, till all the spirit is out of him and he becomes backboneless and 'feeble in the fight'.

GLAUCON. Quite so.

SOCRATES. If, on the other hand, he goes in for hard work in gymnastics only, doesn't the good condition of his body at first make him spirited and fearless? But what is the outcome of keeping on with gymnastics only? Even if he had at the start some taste for music, if that taste is not ever given any food, in knowledge or thought, and he takes no part in discussion or reasoning, doesn't he become unable to take anything in, through having nothing for his mind to do and because his senses are not cleared? Such a man comes to hate thinking, becomes a stranger to the Muses, and gives up the use of reason in getting others to do things. Like an animal, he does everything by rough and violent ways, living without knowledge or measure or grace.

GLAUCON. True.

SOCRATES. To put these two sorts of minds, the spirited and the philosophic, into agreement, some god, I will say, has given man these two arts, music and gymnastics—not (412) for mind and body separately, but for the harmony of the two. And whoever is most able in the use of the two to this end, and in uniting them in it, is most truly named complete in music—not the man who is only good at managing an instrument.

GLAUCON. With good reason, Socrates.

SOCRATES. Then will not such a guardian be necessary at all times in our society, Glaucon, if it is to go on safely?

GLAUCON. Yes, truly we won't be able to do without him.

SOCRATES. Such then will be the outlines of our system of education and training. Why go into details farther? The point for us now is: Which of the persons so trained are to be the rulers and which the ruled? Is there any doubt that the rulers have to be the older men and the best men among them—those most able as guardians of the society? They will be the men with strong minds and great powers, and with the most reason to take care of the state. Won't a man be most careful of what he loves, and will he not probably love most what he believes has the same interests as himself?

GLAUCON. Yes.

SOCRATES. Then after observation we will select from among the body of the guards those who stand out for the care with which, throughout, they have done what seemed to them best for the state, and said 'No' to what seemed to them not good for it.

GLAUCON. Yes. Those are the right persons.

SOCRATES. Let them be watched at every stage to see if they keep a tight grip on this belief that they have to do what is best for the state and aren't ever forced into letting it go.

GLAUCON. What sort of 'letting go' are you talking of?

SOCRATES. Opinions seem to me to go from the mind (413) either with or without our will. When a man sees he's in error he willingly puts the false opinion from him; but a true opinion is only taken away against his will—by arguments or by pain, or fear, or through the attractions of pleasure. And in watching our future rulers, we have to see that they keep their belief and do what is best for the state against all these different forces. We take young horses into noisy places to see what fear does to them. So let us take our young rulers into dangers, and then to places of pleasure—testing them much more completely than gold is tested—to see if they keep control of themselves. Keep true to the music they have been learning and true under all conditions to the laws of rhythm and harmony, acting in all ways so as to be of most use to themselves and to the society. And whoever comes through these tests every time is to be made a guardian (414) and ruler of the society and all others will be turned away.

GLAUCON. I am very much of your opinion.

SOCRATES. Then, Glaucon, is it not right to give to these true and tested men the name of 'guardians'—as being able to see that their friends in the society have no desire, and others outside it have no power, to damage the society? And let the young men we have been naming 'guards' till now, be named 'helpers', because their work is to give support to the decisions of the rulers.

GLAUCON. Quite right.

SOCRATES. If so, how about putting into play one of these medical fictions we were talking about? What if, by one spirited false statement, we might make even the rulers themselves, if possible, believe it—or at least the rest of the society?

GLAUCON. What sort of fiction?

SOCRATES. Nothing unheard of—a Phoenician story which was used of old, as poets say, and they are believed by men. But it is not used now and it's not probable that it will be tried. And it would take more than a little to make anyone give it credit.

GLAUCON. You seem very slow in getting it out.

SOCRATES. Naturally, and you will see why when I do get it out.

GLAUCON. Go on without fear.

SOCRATES. Well, I will. Still I will hardly be able to get the nerve or the words for it. However, I'd attempt first to give the rulers, and the military, and after them the rest, the belief that while we were training them they were in fact sleeping and only dreaming that all this was going on. But in fact they were in the inside of the earth being made and when they were ready the earth, their mother, sent them up and so now they had better take thought first for their country as their mother and nurse, and keep off all attacks on her, and look on the others in their society as their brothers and children of the same earth.

GLAUCON. It wasn't without reason that you were so slow in giving us your fiction!

SOCRATES. Still, let me give you the rest. We will say, in (415) the language of fiction: 'You are, without doubt, all brothers, but the god who made you put gold into the make-up of those who may rightly be guardians, and into the helpers he put silver, but he put iron and brass into the farmers and the workmen. The sons and daughters will generally be like their fathers and mothers, but sometimes a golden mother will have a silver son, or a silver father a golden daughter and so on. The rulers, however, are responsible as watchful guardians for this first to the gods, to see which of those metals has gone into the minds of the young. And if there is brass or iron in one, they have no regret, but give it the value which it naturally has and put it among the farmers and workmen. And if again among these is produced a boy or girl of gold or silver, when tests have been made, they are to put it up among the guardians or the helpers, because the gods have said that the society will come to destruction if it is guarded by iron or brass.' Now, how may we get this fiction to be believed?

GLAUCON. There is no way with the men who are in at the start of our state. But maybe their sons and those who come after will have some belief in it.

SOCRATES. Well, even this might have a good effect in making them care for the state and one another. However, let the fiction go. For our part, after arming these sons of earth, let us take them to the place where the society is to be, under the orders of their rulers, and there choose a strong place for the guards from which to make the rest of the society take their orders, if there are any who have doubts about it, and keep off any attack from without. And when this is done, and offerings have been made to the gods, (416) let them put up their houses. And let them be the houses of men of war, not men of property.

GLAUCON. How are they different?

SOCRATES. I take it that it would be a crime in keepers of sheep to have dogs which attack the sheep themselves and are more like wolves than dogs. And will we not have to take great care that the guards, being stronger than most, don't do so to the citizens?

GLAUCON. We will.

SOCRATES. And won't the only thing which will make us safe against that be the right education for these guards?

GLAUCON. But they have *that* already!

SOCRATES. The right education, my dear Glaucon, will be that which has most effect in making them be gentle to one another and to those they are guarding. And would not reason say that their housing and conditions generally will have to be on such a scale as will let them be good guards and still not give them cause to attack the others?

GLAUCON. Quite so.

SOCRATES. See then if this idea is the right one. In the first place, no one is to have any private property, if that may be possible. Secondly, no one is to have any house or store into which everyone may not go. Whatever is needed by self-controlled and fear-free men, trained for war, is to be given them regularly by the citizens as payment. They are to have their meals together, as men do when at war. As for gold and silver, we will say that as they have these metals forever placed in their souls by the gods themselves, they have no need of either. In fact the touch of either metal would be a danger to them, because money has been the cause of more wrongdoing than may be (417) measured, and their own metal is clean. Therefore they may not put their hands on gold or silver, or let themselves be touched by it, or go under the same roof with it, or have it on their dresses, or use it in cups. Living so, they would save their country and themselves. But whenever they become owners of lands, or houses, or money, then they will become farmers or men of business and not guards, and will come to be against the citizens, not with them. And then they will pass their days, hating and hated, plotting and being plotted against, in more fear of those within than without; by which time they and the rest of the society will be on the very edge of destruction. On all these accounts, we will say that this is the right way of living and the right housing and so on for the guards and make our laws so; or not?

GLAUCON. Yes, in every way.

BOOK IV

ADEIMANTUS. Socrates, how would you answer the charge that you are not making these guardians very happy? The state is theirs, they are its owners in fact; but they get no pleasure from it, as others do, who own lands, build great houses, put all they want in them, make private offerings to the gods and give their friends a good time and have gold and silver and everything which is generally thought necessary if we are to be happy. No, (420) your guardians seem to be stationed in the town like a paid army with nothing to do but keep watch.

SOCRATES. Yes, and for this they get only their food—no money; so that they can't travel or give presents to women or use money for anything else. All that has slipped out of your charge.

ADEIMANTUS. Well, put it all in. What then?

SOCRATES. By going over the same road as before, it seems to me, we will see what to say. Though we wouldn't be surprised if, even under these conditions, our guardians were most happy. And anyhow, we are not separating off a part of the state to be happy but making the state itself happy. If someone came up to us while we were painting a statue and said, 'You are wrong. You haven't put the most beautiful colours on the most beautiful parts of the body. The eyes, the most beautiful part, aren't painted the brightest colour, but black!' wouldn't it be enough of an answer to say, 'Don't let us make these eyes so beautiful that they are no longer eyes, but let us see if, by giving every part its right colour, we may make the whole form beautiful!'? So here, don't let us make these guards anything but guards. Mightn't we, on the same lines, give our farmers long dresses and put crowns on their heads and say, 'Work only when you please!'? Or mightn't we stretch our potters out all day on beds, resting before the fire, with their wheels at their sides, drinking and taking their pleasure, under directions to do their work only while it was an amusement? Might we not hand out this sort of happy existence to all the rest, so that the society might be happy throughout? But don't say we are to do this, because, then, the farmer would (421) be no farmer, the potter no potter, and none of the others who together make up the society would keep his place. In a shoemaker this would not be so serious. But when the guardians of the laws and the state only seem guardians and aren't so in fact, then they will be the destruction, root and branch, of all the rest. We have to make our guardians and helpers such that they become as good at ruling as it is possible to be.

ADEIMANTUS. I think you are right.

SOCRATES. Will the next step seem right too?

ADEIMANTUS. What is it?

SOCRATES. That those in other lines of work, equally, are made worse by two conditions.

ADEIMANTUS. What conditions?

SOCRATES. Wealth and poverty.

ADEIMANTUS. How so?

SOCRATES. Will a potter, after he has become rich, go on giving his mind to making pots?

ADEIMANTUS. Certainly not.

SOCRATES. Won't he do less and take less care than before?

ADEIMANTUS. Yes, much less.

SOCRATES. So, he'll be a worse potter.

ADEIMANTUS. A much worse potter.

SOCRATES. And, on the other hand, if he is so poor that he hasn't the right instruments and materials for his work, he will make worse pots; and his sons and other learners will get worse teaching from him.

ADEIMANTUS. Without doubt.

SOCRATES. Then both these conditions—wealth and poverty (422)—make the produce of the workmen worse and the workmen worse themselves? Because the outcome of the first is loose living, no work and new ways; and the outcome of the other is loss of self-respect, and poor work, and new ways again.

ADEIMANTUS. Quite right!

SOCRATES. We said before that the guardians were to send boys and girls up among the guardians or down among the workers as they saw their quality. That is to be a sign to the other citizens that every one of them is to do the work he is naturally fitted for—not a number of different sorts of work. So, if every man is united within himself (423) (and not a number of different persons), the state too will be united and not a number of different states. And this won't be hard if the guardians keep the one chief thing in view.

ADEIMANTUS. What is that?

SOCRATES. Education and the guiding of growth. For if by education they become men of reason, the guardians will easily understand all these questions, as well as others that we are putting on one side for the present, such as the relations between the sexes, and how they are to be married and the getting of children; in all of which (424) things they will see how wise was the old saying: 'Among friends everything is in common.'

ADEIMANTUS. Yes, that is the right idea.

SOCRATES. If a society has made a good start its growth rolls on, as it were. Good education makes good citizens, and good citizens, helped by good education, become better than they were, handing on better and better natures, as with other animals. But one law our guardians must keep in force, never letting it be overlooked and guarding it with more care than all the rest. This law keeps new ways in music or in gymnastics out of the state which already has its fixed and reasoned order. When men say, 'The new song has the most attraction', it may be thought that we are talking not about new songs but about new ways of making them, and so new ways might seem to be given approval. But new ways are not good and these words are not to be taken as saying that they are. We have to keep new sorts of music away from us as a danger to society; because forms and rhythms in music are never changed without producing changes in the most important political forms and ways; at least, so Damon says, and I am with him.

ADEIMANTUS. Let me in among the believers as well.

SOCRATES. Then it seems that it is here in music that the guardians will build their guardhouse.

ADEIMANTUS. At any rate, it is easiest here for a tendency which is against the law to come in.

SOCRATES. Yes, because it seems to be only amusement, with nothing damaging about it.

ADEIMANTUS. And what damage does it do—but that it quietly, step by step, gets a footing in our ways of living and business? From that it goes over into ways of making and keeping agreements, and from there to attacking public laws and the forms of the state, and this it does without any shame at all, Socrates, till the end is the overturning of everything, public and private.

SOCRATES. Good! Is this so?

ADEIMANTUS. In my view it is.

SOCRATES. Then, from the start, in their earliest play the young will be kept to law and measure through music, (425) because when their play isn't so, it's not possible for them to become serious law-respecting men. But if their amusements are right, their minds become true and in that way anything in the forms of society which may by chance have become bent is made straight again.

ADEIMANTUS. Yes, that's so.

SOCRATES. They will discover again even those little rules of behaviour, as some say they are, which may have been completely dropped by those who went before.

ADEIMANTUS. Which rules are those?

SOCRATES. Those for example which say the young are to keep quiet in the company of older persons, getting up when they come into the room, and giving every attention to their fathers and mothers; together with the rules about how the hair is cut and the forms of dress and shoes and ornaments of the person, and so on. But it would be foolish to make rules about these things. And I would not be for stretching out law-making here to business agreements between private persons, and all the details of taxes and markets, the police and the like. Why give directions on such points to good men, for it won't be hard for them to make all the rules needed themselves? That is, my friend, if they are able, with God's help, to keep the laws of which we *have* been talking.

ADEIMANTUS. If not, they will be always changing the rules, in the hope of somehow getting them right at last.

SOCRATES. Like sick people, with no self-control, who won't give up the habits which are the cause of their troubles!

ADEIMANTUS. Exactly!

SOCRATES. What an existence! Always in the doctor's (426) hands and never getting any better; only adding to their diseases. Still hoping someone will give them something to put them right.

ADEIMANTUS. That's it.

SOCRATES. And don't they hate anyone who says that until they give up their heavy drinking, their great meals, their loose ways, nothing the doctor may do will make them any better? Isn't it a pleasing picture!

ADEIMANTUS. Not so very pleasing; there is nothing pleasing about being angry with someone who says what is true.

SOCRATES. You don't seem to think much of these people.

ADEIMANTUS. I don't.

SOCRATES. When a complete society acts so, isn't it the same? When the form of government is bad, the rulers keep saying to their citizens, 'On pain of death, don't attack the Constitution'. Anyone ready to be their servant, good as any dog at pleasing them, will be said to be deeply wise in political business. Law-making under such conditions (427) is only cutting off the heads of a Hydra.

ADEIMANTUS. That is exactly what it is. As law-makers, then, what more have we to do?

SOCRATES. Nothing more. But for Apollo, the god of Delphi, there is still the ordering of the greatest and highest things of all.

ADEIMANTUS. And what are these?

SOCRATES. Temples and sacrifices and the service of gods and heroes; the burning of the dead and what we should do to be friends with those in the other world. These are matters we do not understand and in founding a city we should, if we are wise, leave all this to Apollo who sits on the omphalos, the mid-point of the world, at Delphi and is the authority on all such things to all mankind.

ADEIMANTUS. Well said. And that we must do.

SOCRATES. Now the organization of our society is complete, son of Ariston: what you have to do is to take a good look at it, under whatever light you are able to get, with the help of your brother and Polemarchus and the rest, in order to see, if you may, where justice comes in it, and where injustice, and how they are different and which of them a man who hopes to be happy will do well to have, whether gods and men know or not!

GLAUCON. No, you don't, Socrates. That won't do. It was you who undertook to go into the question, saying you would be impious if you didn't give us all the help in your power!

SOCRATES. It was as you say. And I will do so, but you will have to do your part.

GLAUCON. We will.

SOCRATES. I am in hopes then we will see what we are looking for in this way. I take it that our state, since it has the right organization, is completely good—therefore wise, brave, temperate, and just?

GLAUCON. Clearly.

SOCRATES. Then, if we see what three of these four virtues (428) in it are, what is left over will be what the other one is! Now this society is wise, isn't it?

GLAUCON. Yes.

SOCRATES. And this wisdom is a certain sort of knowledge—not the knowledge of its carpenters, or any special workers, but of its government, its guardians. Isn't that so?

GLAUCON. Certainly.

SOCRATES. It is the knowledge which its smallest part, (429) the guardians, have about ruling the state which makes it wise. So much for one of our four qualities.

GLAUCON. To my mind, that has been made out all right!

SOCRATES. Again, it is not hard to make out what the quality of being brave is, or where it is to be seen in our state. We'd have our eye on its fighting men, wouldn't we, on the part which takes the field for it. When the right sort of wool has been rightly made ready for dyeing and then is dyed with the true sea-purple, it keeps its colour through every test. So with what we were attempting throughout all our education and training of the guards. It was to (430) put the knowledge of what is truly to be feared into their minds so that it would not be washed out even by forces as strong as pleasure—stronger than any potash or soap—or as strong as pain, fear, and desire, which are stronger than any other undoers on earth. This power, then, I am naming 'courage', if you see nothing against the word.

GLAUCON. Nothing, for though animals and slaves without education may sometimes have the right view on what is to be feared, we would not see that as quite the same thing, and would give it some other name.

SOCRATES. Most true. So take that as our account of the courage of citizens. But now let us go after justice. We have done enough for courage, haven't we?

GLAUCON. You are right.

SOCRATES. Two qualities we still have to find in our society. Temperance, and that which is the cause of all this questioning, justice. So let us give ourselves no more trouble about temperance, but go straight to justice.

GLAUCON. No, go into temperance first.

SOCRATES. Very well. Temperance seems more of a harmony than the other qualities.

GLAUCON. How?

SOCRATES. Temperance, I take it, is a sort of beautiful order, a control, as men say, over certain desires and pleasures. So a man is said to be 'master of himself', a (431) strange way of talking, because, if he is master of himself, he is equally the slave of himself, for it is one and the same person who is being talked of.

GLAUCON. Undoubtedly.

SOCRATES. Well, the sense of this seems to me to be that in the man himself, that is, in his soul, there are two parts or forces, a good one and a bad one. And when the good one has the upper hand and authority then the man is said to be 'master of himself'. These are certainly words of approval. When it's the other way, and the smaller, best part is overruled by the mass of the worse, then he is 'the slave of himself'—certainly not words of approval.

GLAUCON. That seems right enough.

SOCRATES. Now, turn your eyes on our new society. There you will see that the best part is in control of that which is not so good. And these desires and pleasures and pains which have to be kept in control are seen chiefly in the young and in women and servants, and in the masses who are free only in name. But the simple measured desires go hand in hand with thought and right opinion; they are guided by reason, and are found only in a few men of the best natural powers and the best education.

GLAUCON. True.

SOCRATES. You see the parallel on all these accounts with our society which is temperate and master of itself. Again, in our society the rulers and the ruled are of one mind about who gives the orders, so we were not going wrong in saying that temperance was a sort of union and so (432) not quite like wisdom and courage, for they are the qualities of the guardians and of the guards, but this is something uniting the weakest and the strongest and the middle sort, making them all of one mind; so temperance in a society or in a man is a sort of agreement or harmony as to what is to be the government.

GLAUCON. I'm in full agreement with you here.

SOCRATES. So these are three of our qualities, aren't they? What will the fourth one, justice, be? Now, Glaucon, keep a sharp watch, for it is clear that justice is somewhere here. Don't let her get away from us, but if you see her first, cry out.

GLAUCON. Right, but it will be enough if I can see her when you point her out.

SOCRATES. Truly the way is hard and covered with trees, and dark, but we have to go on looking.

GLAUCON. Truly it is, but go on.

SOCRATES. Ho! Ho! Glaucon, here is something like a footprint. Glaucon, in my belief she won't get away.

GLAUCON. Good news!

SOCRATES. Glaucon, we are in a very foolish position.

GLAUCON. How so?

SOCRATES. Why, my dear man, it seems that what we have been looking for so long has all this time been rolling under our feet. And we never saw it. We've been like men looking for something they have in their hands. Instead of fixing our eyes upon the thing itself, we've been looking into the distance, and that is probably why it kept out of view. In my belief, we have been talking of it without taking it in or seeing that we were, all the time, giving a sort of account of it.

GLAUCON. This all seems a bit long-winded when we are waiting for your account.

SOCRATES. Then judge if I'm right or not. (433) What we put forward at the very start as the first principle of our society, this, if I'm not wrong now, this or some form of it, is justice. Didn't we say that everyone was to have some one special sort of work in the society, the work which he was naturally most able to do?

GLAUCON. We did say so.

SOCRATES. It would seem that minding one's own business and not putting one's fingers into other men's work is, in some form or other, justice. Do you see why?

GLAUCON. No. Do make it clearer.

SOCRATES. This last virtue is what makes the growth of the other virtues possible in the political body and, while it is present, it keeps them safe. See here! In our state, the judges will be guided by the idea that no one is to get (434) what is another's, because that isn't just. And by this view to have and do what is ours and our business, is just?

GLAUCON. True.

SOCRATES. Now see if you are with me here. If a carpenter undertakes a shoemaker's work, is the state much damaged?

GLAUCON. Not much.

SOCRATES. But when a person who is by nature only a worker or producer of some sort gets so above himself—through having important relations, or a strong body, or much property—as to push himself in among the military guards; or when a guard gets himself made a guardian when he is not good enough, or when the same man undertakes to do everything, then that sort of thing *does* put the state in danger.

GLAUCON. Certainly.

SOCRATES. Now *that* is injustice. And when the workers, the military and the guardians keep to their own work—the work they are naturally fitted for—*that* is justice and that makes the society just.

GLAUCON. I am with you fully.

SOCRATES. Let's not be over-certain but test this idea on the one man by himself and see if this is justice in him. If not, we will look for something different. For we have been attempting to see first what justice is in some large-scale example of it, with the idea that it would then be less hard to see it in one man. And this great example was our state to which we gave the best organization we could—knowing that justice would have to be present in a good society. Now let us go back to the one man (435) by himself; if we rub the two examples together, maybe justice, like fire from two sticks rubbed together, will come into view—to be fixed ever after in ourselves.

GLAUCON. That seems right. Let's do so!

SOCRATES. When two things rightly have the same name, are they like or unlike?

GLAUCON. Like.

SOCRATES. Then a just man and a just state, so far as the idea of justice comes in, will be alike. Now we have said the state is just when the three sorts of people in it do their right work; and that it is temperate, brave and wise through certain qualities and conditions of these three sorts of citizens.

GLAUCON. Right.

SOCRATES. Then the just man will have to have in his soul the same three forms; and he will be just, temperate, brave, and wise only through qualities and conditions of these forms which are the same as with the state—if the same words are rightly to be used of him.

GLAUCON. There is no way out of that!

SOCRATES. Here is another little question we have come upon! The structure of the soul: has it these three forms in it or not?

GLAUCON. A little question! But maybe, Socrates, it is true that the beautiful is hard?

SOCRATES. It would seem so. But I may as well say to you, Glaucon, here and now, that in my view we won't ever get a completely true answer to all this by the ways we've been using in this discussion. However, the road that would take us to *that* is over-long and over-hard. And maybe we'll get a true enough answer this way. Will that do? It would do for me for the present.

GLAUCON. And for me. So go on.

SOCRATES. Is it possible to say we haven't in us the same (436) three parts we saw in the state? For if not, where did the state get them from? But here comes the hard point. Are all our acts equally the work of the same thing in us? Or are there three things working separately in our different acts? Is learning the work of one, and becoming angry the work of another, and do we, with a third, desire the pleasures of food and drink and the getting of offspring? Or, in all that we do is the whole soul always acting? What is hard is to get these points fixed and clear enough.

GLAUCON. I'd say it was!

SOCRATES. How about this line of attack? It is clear that the same thing isn't able to do two opposite things at the same time, or be in two opposite conditions—in the same respects, that is, and with relation to the same other thing. So, when we see two opposite things being done, we may be certain that two or more things are doing them, not one and the same thing.

GLAUCON. Very well.

SOCRATES. Now, your best attention, please.

GLAUCON. You have it; go on.

SOCRATES. Is it possible for the same thing to be, at the same time, and in the same respects, at rest and in motion?

GLAUCON. Certainly not.

SOCRATES. Good, but to keep ourselves from being troubled by doubts later note that a man may be at rest but moving his hands about. And that a top, or any other thing which is only turning round and round, may be said to be in one place, that is, at rest, though it is moving. So, not to give time to all such examples and the (437–8) arguments from them, let us take it that it's not possible for one and the same thing to be itself and the opposite, or to produce two opposite effects or be acted upon in two opposite ways—at the same time and from the same point of view, and in relation to the same other thing.

GLAUCON. Right.

SOCRATES. And if ever we take a different view on this, all our decisions based on this view will go down. Among opposites are: saying 'Yes' to something and saying 'No', going after something and keeping it off, attraction and pushing away. Wouldn't you agree?

GLAUCON. I would.

SOCRATES. And wouldn't you put all desires for food or drink or whatever it be under the head of attraction or 'Yes' saying? Every desire seems to go after something or attempts to get it with a sort of pull. In desiring something, don't we, as it were, say 'Yes' to it, as if it were a question? And disgust and opposition you'll put under the head of saying 'No'.

GLAUCON. Certainly.

SOCRATES. Well now, take a man when thirst is driving (439) him like a beast to drink. If anything in his soul pulls him back from drinking it will be something different and separate from that which is desiring the drink, won't it—because it is not possible for the same thing to do two opposite things?

GLAUCON. Certainly.

SOCRATES. So there is no account to be given of such men but this. That their minds have one form which says, 'Drink', and another which says, 'No, don't!' and the second is different from and able to master the first. And whenever such an authority comes to full growth in the mind, it is the offspring of reason, while the other comes from disease?

GLAUCON. It would seem so.

SOCRATES. So we have a good argument for saying there are two powers in the mind, and for naming one of them by which it thinks 'reason'; the other, which is moved by hunger and thirst and love, as a bird is moved by its wings, is 'desire'. But now, will spirit, or that with which we become angry, be a third power in the mind?

GLAUCON. Maybe it is the same as desire in some way.

SOCRATES. But there is a story I heard of Leontius, son of Aglaïon: as he was walking up from the Peiraeus here near the outside of the north wall, he saw some dead bodies at the place of execution. He felt a very strong desire to have a look at them, but was disgusted with himself (440) for feeling it. He fought with himself and covered his eyes, but in the end, overpowered by the desire, he went running up to them, his eyes wide open, crying, 'There, you good-for-nothings, fill yourselves with this beautiful sight!'

GLAUCON. I have heard that story too.

SOCRATES. There is a suggestion in it that angry feelings sometimes go against the desires. If so, they are different. And haven't you very frequently seen a man who is overcome by his desires get angry with them and their violent way of working in him? That is, spirit takes the side of reason? But for spirit to make common cause with the desires, when reason is against them, that you won't have seen. That isn't in our experience.

GLAUCON. No.

SOCRATES. Then our idea that the spirit went along with desire was wrong. Much more readily it takes up arms for reason. But is it a third thing in the mind, separate from reason and desire? And may we say that as the state is made up of and kept together by the three great orders, (441) so in the mind the spirit is a third form, which naturally supports reason, if it is not diseased through ill-training?

GLAUCON. It's a third thing.

SOCRATES. Yes, if it's different from reason and different from desire.

GLAUCON. That is not hard to make out, for, even in the young, from their very birth there is spirit; but reason is something most men only get after a number of years and some don't get it ever, in my opinion.

SOCRATES. Well said. Here then, after a long and hard journey, we come to land. There are these three sorts in the mind like the three sorts in the state, and a man by himself is wise and brave as a state is wise and brave. And he is just in the same way that a state is just.

GLAUCON. Yes!

SOCRATES. Let us keep in mind that what makes a state (442–3) just is everybody doing his right work. In every one of us, if everything does *its* right work, that will make us just and make us do *our* right work! Is that a good enough account of justice?

GLAUCON. It is.

SOCRATES. And injustice? As the opposite of justice, it (444) will be a condition of war between these three things, which get in each other's way. It will be an attempt by the lower to give orders to the higher, the reason. From which doings the soul becomes unjust, feeble, loose, full of fears, uncontrolled, foolish, and, in a word, diseased. For all this in the mind is completely parallel to what takes place in the body, isn't it?

GLAUCON. How's that?

SOCRATES. By being healthy we keep healthy, don't we? But disease makes a man diseased. In the same way justice—ruled by knowledge—keeps us just, but injustice—ruled by ignorance—makes us unjust. Now the way to become healthy is to let the forces of the body control, and be controlled by, one another in the natural way. But disease is produced by one of them overruling others against the natural order. So it is with justice and injustice (445) in the mind. Now is there any need to ask, 'Does justice give a profit?'?

GLAUCON. No, Socrates. Now that we know what justice and injustice are, that question seems foolish. What! Don't we agree that when the constitution of the body is broken down, it is no good going on living any longer? And when the very balance of forces by which we live is overturned, is anything worth doing except what will free us from evil and put back some measure of justice in our hearts?

SOCRATES. That is right. But from this high point in the argument like watchmen we may see that there is one form of virtue, but any number of forms of evil, of which four are specially in need of being noted.

GLAUCON. Why four?

SOCRATES. It would seem that the sorts of minds are parallel with the sorts of societies. And there are five forms of governments and five different sorts of minds.

GLAUCON. Which are they?

SOCRATES. One form of government is the one we have been giving an account of, and it may have two different names. If among the guardians there is one man better far than the rest, let it be named a monarchy; if the best are more than one, let it be an aristocracy. But it is still one form: for whether one man rules or a number rule will not be important; the laws of the society will not be changed, if their education and training are as in our account.

GLAUCON. Probably not.

BOOK V

SOCRATES. Such a state then, and the parallel sort of man, I name good and right; but the others are bad and wrong, and of these there are four chief forms.

GLAUCON. Which are they?

SOCRATES. What is all this, Polemarchus? Why are you pulling at Adeimantus and whispering in his ear?

POLEMARCHUS. Is he to be let off, Adeimantus?

ADEIMANTUS. On no account.

SOCRATES. Who is not to be let off what?

ADEIMANTUS. You.

SOCRATES. What about?

ADEIMANTUS. You are not doing your work. You are attempting to dodge a very important part of the argument, to save yourself the trouble of going into it. Did you hope to slip away from us by lightly saying that everyone will see that the rule, 'Among friends everything is in common', will cover women and children as well?

SOCRATES. But isn't that right, Adeimantus?

ADEIMANTUS. Yes, but this word 'right', like other things, needs going into here. How are they to be in common? There might be numbers of ways. We've been waiting a long time for you to take up the question of the family and this business of women being in common. (450) It may make things very different; so now, if you are starting on another form of government before you've completed this one, we have made up our minds, as you heard, not to let you go till you have said as much about this side of it as you did about the rest.

GLAUCON. I agree.

THRASYMACHUS. We are of one mind on this.

SOCRATES. You've done it now! What an argument you are starting about our republic! And I was so pleased at completing it, and having your agreement as I got it out. You little see what a cloud of hornet-words you are getting us into. I saw how it would be and kept out of it for fear of no end of trouble.

THRASYMACHUS. Well, what did we come here for—to look for gold or to have a discussion?

SOCRATES. Yes, a discussion within limits.

GLAUCON. No, Socrates, the limit of such a discussion, for a wise man, is all his days. So don't mind about us, and don't get tired yourself; but give us your views on how the guardians and guards are to have their women and children in common, and about the care of the very young, which is thought to be the hardest part of education.

SOCRATES. It is not a light thing to talk about, no lighter than what went before it, for more doubts come up. One may doubt if my suggestion would work, or if it's the best thing. And so I have kept off it for fear it is only a hope, my friend.

GLAUCON. Don't, for your hearers won't be hard on you. They are not unbelieving, or hostile.

SOCRATES. My good Glaucon. Is that said to encourage me?

GLAUCON. It is.

SOCRATES. Well it has the very opposite effect. If I were certain about all this it *would* give me courage. For to say what one really knows about our dearest and greatest interests to those who are wise and dear is safe and easy enough. But to say what one doubts, what one is looking for as one talks, as I am doing now, is a fearful thing. (451) And the fear isn't of being laughed at—that's for babies only—but that I'll go wrong and take my friends with me into error about the very things it is most important not to go wrong about. May Nemesis not overtake me for what I am about to say. This is a danger better run among enemies than among friends.

GLAUCON. All right, Socrates. If anything false in the argument damages us, you are freed from all charges. It won't be on *your* head. So go on without fear.

SOCRATES. Then let us go back. The part of the men has been

played and now comes the turn of the women. From the start we were attempting to make our guards good watchdogs. Let us work out this comparison and then see if it is right.

GLAUCON. How?

SOCRATES. Do female watchdogs work with the males, or are they kept indoors, as being unable to do their part because they produce young, while the male dogs work and care for all?

GLAUCON. They do all things in common. Only the females are not so strong as the males.

SOCRATES. If women are to do the same things as (452) men, we will have to give them the same training, that is, music and gymnastics and offices of war. And wouldn't that make some men laugh?

GLAUCON. It certainly would.

SOCRATES. The very idea of women wearing armour and riding on horseback! And the thing which will be laughed at most, wouldn't it be the thought of the women doing their gymnastics naked with the men; not only the young ones but the older ones as well, like the old men who keep on exercising though their bodies are not what you would most want to look at?

GLAUCON. Yes, that would be laughed at under present conditions.

SOCRATES. Let us request these laughers to be serious this time. Not very long ago, if they will stretch their memories, even the Greeks thought it shameful to be seen without clothes on, and other countries still have that idea. When the Cretans first and then the Lacedaemonians began to exercise naked did not the funny-men have a fine chance? But when experience had shown that it is better not to be covered, men got used to what reason saw was best. Only what is wrong is to be laughed at; the only measure of the beautiful is the good.

GLAUCON. Certainly.

SOCRATES. The first thing is to see if these suggestions (453) are possible. Who doubts, seriously or not, if a woman is able to take part in men's work, some of it or all of it, and where war comes in here? Isn't that the best way to start—the way which will take us to the best end, as the saying is?

GLAUCON. Far the best.

SOCRATES. Let us take up the two sides of the argument, like this: 'Socrates and Glaucon, you yourselves, at the start, said, "Everyone is to keep to his own business."' 'We did.' 'Well, aren't men and women very different?' 'They are.' 'Why do you turn round now and say men and women are to do the same things, though they are naturally so different?' Now, Glaucon, will you surprise me with an answer to that?

GLAUCON. Not straightaway. It comes so suddenly. But do let us have your answer to it, whatever it is.

SOCRATES. These are the hard points, Glaucon, which I saw waiting for us, when I kept away from touching on the laws about women and children. These and others like them.

GLAUCON. It is hard, by Zeus!

SOCRATES. Why yes, but the fact is that when we fall into deep water, we have to swim for it whether it's a pool we are in or the great sea. So let's swim out of this sea of argument, and get to land again. A great thing, (454) Glaucon, is this power of making one say opposite things.

GLAUCON. Why do you say that?

SOCRATES. Because it seems to me that many men fall into its hands against their will. They take themselves to be reasoning when they are only mixing things up, in a fighting spirit, through not being able to use the right divisions of the forms; and they make opposites of *things* when it is only the *words* which are opposite, and go in for eristic, word-fighting—not dialectic.

GLAUCON. Yes, that's so, but is it true of us here now?

SOCRATES. Certainly. I fear, at least, we are slipping unconsciously into word-fighting.

GLAUCON. In what way?

SOCRATES. We are keeping most manfully and in a fine fighting spirit to the wording of the law that beings who are not the same are not to do the same work; but did we stop to see in what ways they were to be 'the same' when we handed out different work to different men and the same to the same?

GLAUCON. No, we didn't go into that.

SOCRATES. For example, are bald men and long-haired men the same? No? Then if bald men make shoes, are we to stop long-haired ones from doing so?

GLAUCON. That would be foolish.

SOCRATES. And why? For any other reason than that we haven't *any and every way* of being different in view, but only those which have some effect on the work the men do? For example, a man and a woman equally medical-minded will be, as far as medical things go, the same. But a medical man and a carpenter will be different. So, if it seems that the male and the female sex have different qualities making them good at different arts or forms of work, then we will say they are to do different things. But if they seem different only in this: that the female produces and the male begets, we will say that no argument has been made out and we will go on giving our guardians and these women the same work to do.

GLAUCON. Rightly.

SOCRATES. Now let us request whoever is of another (455) opinion to say for which of the arts of ruling a state a woman is naturally different from a man. Maybe he would say, as you were saying but now, that this is a hard one to answer suddenly; but that with more time for thought it would not be hard.

GLAUCON. Maybe he would.

SOCRATES. Let us put this question to him. How are you separating the naturally able man from the less able? The one learns readily, the other finds it hard; the one with a little teaching sees much for himself, the other after long training doesn't even keep what he has learned in his head; the one has a body which is a good servant to his mind, the other's body gets in his way. Are there any other differences?

GLAUCON. No one will name any others.

SOCRATES. Is there anything at which the male sex isn't better than the female on all these points? Need we take time arguing about cloth-making, and the watching of cakes and the boiling pot, where it is the woman who will be laughed at if she doesn't do as well as a man?

GLAUCON. You are right to say that the male sex is far better at almost everything than the female. There are women who are better than most men in all sorts of things, but in general it is as you say.

SOCRATES. Then there is nothing in the work of a state which is naturally a woman's work, hers because she is a woman; and nothing which is a man's work, his because he is a man. The same gifts are distributed among them both and there are women and men naturally fitted for each sort of work—but, for all that, women are less strong than men.

GLAUCON. Certainly.

SOCRATES. Then are we to give all the work to the men and none to the women? No, we'll say, I take it, that one woman has a medical bent and another not or one is good at music and another not? Or that one woman is naturally athletic and warlike and another is not warlike and has no taste for gymnastics? Or that one loves and another (456) hates knowledge? Or that one is high-spirited and another without spirit? If so, women may have the qualities which make a good guardian, though men are stronger. Such women are to be taken into the company of the guardians, living in the same common houses and guarding the state with them, and they are to have the same education.

GLAUCON. The same.

SOCRATES. Then, it seems, our suggestion was not impossible, or only a hope. In fact, the other way of doing things, which is current today, is what is unnatural. Ours would be in harmony with the natural order.

GLAUCON. So it seems.

SOCRATES. Well, that gets us through one of the waves (457) in these troubled waters we are swimming in, and we have not been quite pushed under for saying that there are to be men and women guardians with their work in common.

GLAUCON. It is not a little wave that you are getting away from.

SOCRATES. It won't seem a great one when you see what is coming.

GLAUCON. Let us see it. Say on.

SOCRATES. All that has gone before was on the way to this: These best of the women are all to be common to all these best of the men, and their children are to be common, and no father or mother is to have any knowledge as to which of them is his own or any child know who its parents were.

GLAUCON. This is a far greater troublemaker than the other and there will be more doubt about its being possible or useful.

SOCRATES. I take it there would be no argument about its value; no one could say that it wasn't the very best thing, if he took it to be possible. This last is the point there will be trouble about.

GLAUCON. No, you have to face attacks on both points.

SOCRATES. Is it so? I hoped I would get out of the first. (458) Well, let me do as daydreamers do. They don't wait to work out *how* to make their hopes come true, but give themselves up to picturing all the details. What pleasure they get out of seeing what they will do when it has all come about! So their souls, which never did much, come to do less still. But let me be like them while I try to make you see that all this would be the very best thing of all for the state and its guardians. After that I'll come back to how it would be possible.

GLAUCON. You may go on.

SOCRATES. Well now, you, as the lawgiver, have made your selection of these men and women. They have houses and meals in common; no one has anything that is specially his or her own, they are always meeting in their education and in gymnastics, all their ways are together; so necessarily they will unite. Is 'necessarily' an over-strong word here?

GLAUCON. It won't be *geometrically* necessary—but necessary in another way, one that lovers know, far stronger and with more attraction for the masses.

SOCRATES. True enough; but note now, Glaucon, all will be well ordered in these things and all the rest; there will be no loose doings in this happy society. These rulers won't let them in.

GLAUCON. No, it would not be right.

SOCRATES. Clearly, there will have to be public marriages (459) with a holy form and those would be most holy which had the best outcome. So how would we get the best outcome? Glaucon, you have a great number of dogs and birds in your house. Don't you get the best offspring only by uniting the best? And isn't it so with horses and other animals?

GLAUCON. It would be strange if it were not.

SOCRATES. My word, our rulers will need the highest art if it's the same with men and women.

GLAUCON. Certainly it's the same; but where does the art come in?

SOCRATES. Our rulers will have to make no small number of false statements here for the good of the citizens. Didn't we say these might be used by rulers as a sort of medical step?

GLAUCON. And rightly.

SOCRATES. They will have somehow to get the best men married to the best women as frequently as possible, and the worst to the worst as infrequently as may be, so that the offspring of the best may be increased. And knowledge of how this is done will be kept from all but the rulers, if the group of guardians is to be as free as possible from storms. Something will have to be done so that (460) the worse, who don't get the best mates, will put it down to chance and not make the rulers responsible. There would be some sort of lottery perhaps. Those who do best in war or in other things might be married more frequently so that we have more of the best offspring from them. The number of marriages is for the guardians to decide, to keep the number of citizens in the state as nearly as possible the same. The children of the worse fathers and mothers, or any of the others that are diseased, will be put away secretly, and no one will know what has become of them.

GLAUCON. That is to keep up the quality of the guardians' offspring.

SOCRATES. As to nursing, the mothers will do so while they have milk, but every care will be taken to keep them from seeing which are their children. And the mothers aren't to nurse them long, and all the trouble of nights without sleep and such things will be taken over by the public nurses.

GLAUCON. You are not making it very hard work to be a mother.

SOCRATES. And rightly. But any offspring whose birth (461) is against the law is to be done away with.

GLAUCON. All this sounds like reason. But how are they to know who are whose fathers and daughters and so on?

SOCRATES. They won't. A man will name all the males born between the seventh and tenth month after he was married his sons, and all the females his daughters, and they will name him father. And all the offspring of that time will be brothers and sisters. But these brothers and sisters may be married if the Delphic oracle has nothing against it.

GLAUCON. All right.

SOCRATES. That, Glaucon, is the way things would be among the guardians. That it goes with the rest, and is (462) by far the best way, is the next point. And the first step to agreement on that will be to take thought upon what the greatest good for a state is, and the greatest evil, and see if these suggestions don't walk in the footprints of the good?

GLAUCON. Let's see how.

SOCRATES. Is there any worse ill for a state than to be divided or a greater good than being united? And are not pleasure and pain in common the things which unite us, when, so far as may be, all the citizens are happy and unhappy together at the same events? And the chief cause of being separate comes when the citizens don't all say the words 'mine' and 'not mine' of the same things. But when they all do this then the state is most like one man. If one finger is wounded, the complete system of connections stretching from it to the controlling soul undergoes the pain together and we say the man has the pain, though it is only his finger which is damaged. So again with his pleasures.

GLAUCON. The best state is the one which comes nearest to having such an organization.

SOCRATES. When any one citizen experiences some good or ill chance, the whole society will make the joy or grief its own, naming it 'mine'.

GLAUCON. In our society, everyone will all the time be (463–5) meeting a brother, a sister, a father, a mother, a son, or a daughter in everyone he comes across.

SOCRATES. Very good, but it will not be only these *names* he uses to them but the acts and behaviour as well. And the cause of that will be this way of having women and children in common.

GLAUCON. Certainly it will be the chief cause.

SOCRATES. And having all these feelings in common and being free from all the causes of division between men and all the little cares of keeping a private family together, getting enough money for it, and so on, won't they live more happily than even those who are now thought happiest—the victors at Olympia? For the reward of these is to be saviours of the state. Someone went for me earlier for not making the guardians happy. (See 419.)

GLAUCON. That comes back to me.

SOCRATES. Well, now you see what the existence of our (466) rulers will be like. And if some guardian with a child's idea of how to be happy does attempt to use his power to take everything for himself, he will not be long in finding out how truly wise Hesiod was in saying that the half is in some sort more than the whole.

GLAUCON. If he would be guided by me, he'd keep to this way of living.

SOCRATES. So you are in agreement, are you, about all this?

GLAUCON. I am in agreement.

SOCRATES. Then this is the last point: Is this thing possible?

GLAUCON. That is the very question I was about to put.

SOCRATES. For as to their ways in war, that is clear and needs no discussion.

GLAUCON. Is it?

SOCRATES. Yes, it is clear that men and women will go to the wars together, and what is more, take their children (467–9) with them, so that they, like the children of other workers, will see how the work is done. Haven't you noted how the sons of potters look on at their fathers' work? And when it comes to fighting, every animal does best when its offspring is present.

GLAUCON. But the danger, Socrates, is not little.

SOCRATES. But is to keep out of danger the chief thing?

GLAUCON. No, it isn't at all.

SOCRATES. And if they do go into danger isn't it for something which will make them better? And won't seeing the wars when young make them better fighters later? Moreover, the fathers will be good judges of where the danger is. Let them put the children on good horses so that they may get away quickly if things go wrong. And (470–1) in war let there be no burning of fields and houses. The victors may take away the grain, but their behaviour is to be that of men expecting to be friends again with the enemy sometime. It is always a few who cause a war. Let our republic fight on till the prayers of the innocent force the guilty to do justice.

GLAUCON. I agree. But, Socrates, if you go on like this about war, you will never get to the last point: Is this having everything in common possible? I agree that everything would be as good as may be in any state that had it, and I'll make one addition to what you've been saying. They would do very well in war. With the women present, nothing would stop them. I give you all these points, so don't talk on about how good it all would be, but simply let us see if it is possible and how it is to come about.

SOCRATES. This is a sudden attack. I have hardly got (472) through the first two waves, when here comes this 'great third wave' as they say, rolling over me, and it is the worst of all. When you have seen and heard what it is, you will be gentler with me. You'll know what good reason I had for keeping out of a discussion of such troublemaking ideas.

GLAUCON. The more you go on like this, the less we will let you off saying how it's possible. So, no more of it.

SOCRATES. It was a question about justice that got us here.

GLAUCON. Yes, but what of that?

SOCRATES. Oh, only that if we do see what justice is, will our just man have to be completely just or will it do if he is more just than other men?

GLAUCON. That will do.

SOCRATES. It was an example that we were looking for in our questions about justice and about the completely just man, if he has any existence. And so again with injustice, and the completely unjust man. We were to look at them as examples by which to judge how happy or unhappy we are, through being like them. We didn't have to prove that there are in fact such completely just men.

GLAUCON. That is true.

SOCRATES. Would a painter be any the worse if, after painting a picture of a completely beautiful man, he wasn't able to prove that such a man is possible?

GLAUCON. By Zeus, no.

SOCRATES. Weren't we attempting with our words to paint a good state as an example?

GLAUCON. Certainly.

SOCRATES. Then is what we have said any the worse because we are unable to prove that a state may have such a government?

GLAUCON. Not a bit.

SOCRATES. That then is the true position. Now if I am to say under what conditions we might most probably get such a government, answer me this again.

GLAUCON. What?

SOCRATES. Can anything be, in act and fact, as perfect as it is in words; or does fact necessarily come short of language, (473) even though some think this not so?

GLAUCON. Fact comes short.

SOCRATES. Then don't say I'm to put before you as a fact something completely like the account we have given in words. If we are only able to see how a state may be *nearly* as we said, you'll have your example. Would that be enough for you? It would be for me.

GLAUCON. And for me as well.

SOCRATES. What is the smallest change that would give a society this form of government? There is one which would do it, not a little thing and hard enough but still possible.

GLAUCON. What is it?

SOCRATES. Now I'm on the very edge of the greatest of the waves. But I will say it, though it washes me away and crushes me under the laugh. Give ear!

GLAUCON. Say on.

SOCRATES. Till philosophers become kings, or those now named kings and rulers give themselves to philosophy truly and rightly, and these two things—political power and philosophic thought—come together, and the commoner minds, which at present seek only the one or the other, are kept out by force, states will have no rest from their troubles, dear Glaucon, and, if I am right, man will have none. Only then will this our republic see the light of day. That is what I have been so slow about; I knew it would be too strange, for it is hard to see that there is no other way for men to be happy in public or in private life.

GLAUCON. Socrates, if you will fire a statement like that at us, what hope is there that numbers of very solid authorities (474) won't off with their coats, take the first thing to hand, and go for you with all their force, ready to do fearful things? And if you haven't arguments to put up against them and don't get out of it somehow, then you are in for it all right, and to be shamed will be your punishment.

SOCRATES. You got me into this.

GLAUCON. And I was right. But I'll do what I may for you and give you what help I have—that is, good will and encouragement; and I might answer your questions with more care than another. And now, with such a helper, do your best to make the unbelievers see that you are right.

SOCRATES. Don't we need, for that, to mark out for the unbelievers who the philosophers are who are to rule? Then it will be seen that there are some who are naturally fitted to be philosophers and to rule, and others who had better touch neither.

GLAUCON. Let's have a statement of your sense of 'philosopher' then.

SOCRATES. Look in your memory, and see if, when we say a man is a lover of something, the sense is that he loves all of it, not that he loves one part of it and not another.

GLAUCON. You'll have to help my memory, for I don't see the point at all.

SOCRATES. Another person might answer so, but not you. A lover like you will be clear that all beautiful young things have their attraction. However different, there is something about every one of them which a lover of the young turns his attention to.

GLAUCON. If it will help this argument for me to be an (475) authority on that, so be it.

SOCRATES. Is not the same thing true of lovers of wine? They see some reason for taking any sort of wine.

GLAUCON. They do, truly.

SOCRATES. And men who love high position, if they aren't able to head an army, are willing to head a company; if they are not respected by great and important persons, they are happy to be looked up to by little men and nobodies.

GLAUCON. Right.

SOCRATES. Now take my question again: Does a man, who desires some good, desire all sorts of it or only a part?

GLAUCON. All sorts of it.

SOCRATES. Then the lover of wisdom, won't we say, desires not only something of it, but all of it?

GLAUCON. Yes, that is so.

SOCRATES. And whoever has no love for learning, specially when he is young, when he has no power to judge by reason what is useful and what is not, he, we will say, is not a philosopher or friend of wisdom. But whoever has a taste for every sort of knowledge, and desires to learn and never has enough of it, may be named a philosopher. Am I right?

GLAUCON. You will be giving this name to any number of strange beings, for all the lovers of surprising sights are what they are through the pleasure they take in learning something. And those who always hope to hear some new thing are a bit out of place among the philosophers. They are the last persons who would come to a serious discussion, if they might get out of it. No, they go running about to every Dionysiac meeting, as if they had let their ears out to every song. Wherever the music is, there they are. Are we to name all these and the like, and all who go in for the lesser arts as well, all philosophers?

SOCRATES. Not at all, but they are, in one way, a bit like philosophers.

GLAUCON. Who then are the true philosophers?

SOCRATES. Those who are in love with seeing what is true.

GLAUCON. Good, but in what sense do you say that?

SOCRATES. It would be hard to make it clear to another, but you will see this—

GLAUCON. What?

SOCRATES. That if the beautiful is the opposite of the ugly, (476) they are two.

GLAUCON. Certainly.

SOCRATES. So the beautiful is one and the ugly is one. And of the just and the unjust, the good and the bad, and of all the Ideas or Forms, the same is true: each is one; but when joined with acts and bodies and with one another, as seen everywhere, each seems many.

GLAUCON. Very true.

SOCRATES. This then is how I separate the lovers of the things to be seen and heard, and of the arts, from those who alone are rightly named philosophers.

GLAUCON. How do you separate them?

SOCRATES. These lovers of sounds and sights enjoy beautiful voices and colours and outlines, and everything art makes out of these, but their thought is unable to take in and delight in the being of the beautiful itself.

GLAUCON. Yes, that is so.

SOCRATES. But, on the other hand, those able to come near to the beautiful itself and see it for what it is are few.

GLAUCON. Very few.

SOCRATES. He then who believes in beautiful things, but not in that through which they are beautiful, and, if another points out the way to a knowledge of that, is unable to take it, is he awake or dreaming? Think! is not the dream condition, asleep or awake, a copying of what *is* by something which only *seems*?

GLAUCON. Yes, I'd certainly say dreaming was that.

SOCRATES. The opposite man, who knows in his thought that there is beauty in itself and is able to view it, itself, and the things which take part in it—without mistaking it for them or them for it—is such a man sleeping or awake?

GLAUCON. He is very much awake.

SOCRATES. Then may we not name his way of thought, *knowledge*, and that of the dreamer, *opinion*?

GLAUCON. Certainly.

SOCRATES. Knowledge and opinion are different and have (477–9) to do with different things—knowledge with that which *is* and opinion with that which is between being and not-being. So the views of the many about beauty and justice are opinion. Those who, though they view any number of beautiful things, are not able to see what the beautiful itself is, or be guided to it by another, who view just things but cannot see what justice itself is—such men, we'll say, have opinions about all things but no knowledge. But those who look upon the very things themselves, which are ever the same and unchanged, have knowledge and not only opinion.

GLAUCON. That is necessarily so.

SOCRATES. One man welcomes and loves the things of knowledge and another those of opinion. Only those who in each thing love its true being may be named friends of wisdom, or philosophers, not friends of opinion.

GLAUCON. Certainly.

BOOK VI

SOCRATES. And now, Glaucon, which of these two should (484–5) be the chiefs of a state: the blind or those who see clearly; the ignorant or those able to look into the true being of the beautiful, the just and the good, and so order the state? Which should be our guardians?

GLAUCON. It would be strange to take any but the philosophers if they were as experienced and as virtuous as the others.

SOCRATES. If we agree enough about what they naturally must be by birth we will see that all these qualities can be united in the same persons and that we need no other guardians.

GLAUCON. How is that?

SOCRATES. The philosopher is always in love with knowledge of the unchanging. And he will desire all that is knowledge, and hate all that is false.

GLAUCON. Probably.

SOCRATES. Necessarily, my friend, for whoever is in love with anything loves what is like it. The lover of wisdom must all his life desire every form of truth.

GLAUCON. Right.

SOCRATES. When the desire for one sort of thing is strong, desires for other things become weaker—as if the river were turned into another bed. The true philosopher will be temperate and have no great desire for money; the things which others desire money for will not be serious (486) interests to him. And here is another mark. There is nothing small about him. That does not go with seeing things whole. Nor will a mind used to thoughts of the greatest things, used to looking out on all time and all being, take this life of man very seriously. So he will not see death as anything much to be feared.

GLAUCON. He least of all.

SOCRATES. Will such a man be unjust or hard on others?

GLAUCON. Impossible.

SOCRATES. So among the signs of the philosophic soul, see if a man is gentle and just from his earliest days or violent and unable to get on with other men.

GLAUCON. Certainly.

SOCRATES. And don't overlook another point. Is he quick to learn? Is learning a pleasure to him or not? Will anyone work well if he takes no pleasure in it, or if nothing comes of the work? Again, if he has a bad memory and keeps nothing of what he has learned, will he know anything? Having done all *that* for nothing, he will be forced at the last to hate himself and the work. Never list such a man among philosophers, for they have to have strong minds, a natural measure and grace, and be readily guided to the view of true being itself. But don't all these things go (487) together? Is there anything wrong then with philosophy, if a man, to be a philosopher, has to have a good memory, be quick to learn, be great-minded, graceful and of a like kind with and a friend to whatever is true, brave, just, and temperate?

GLAUCON. Momus, himself, would not see anything wrong with that.

SOCRATES. Well then, when men of this sort have come to their full growth through education and years, why not hand the government over to them?

ADEIMANTUS. No one, Socrates, will attack any one of these points of yours. But, all the same, when you argue this way those who hear you feel like this: They believe that—with their small experience in putting and answering questions—they are being led a little bit out of the straight line at every step of the argument, and when these bits are all added together at the end of the discussion, great is their fall—they seem to be saying the opposite of what they said at first. And, as players who are not good at checkers are shut in at last by the expert and are without a move to make, so, in this other sort of checkers, which is played with words, not with bits of wood, they are shut up and haven't a thing to say; and yet they feel that all this has to do with the words only and that they are still in fact in the right. I say this with the present discussion in view. For any one of us might be unable to resist you in words, question by question, but when it comes to facts, many will say that those who go in for philosophy—not as a mere part of education dropped while they are still young but seriously—become, most of them, very strange indeed, not to say rogues, and even the best of them become quite useless to the state through the very thing you have been praising.

SOCRATES. Well, and do you think those who say so are wrong?

ADEIMANTUS. I'm not certain. But I would be happy to hear your opinion.

SOCRATES. Hear then that in my view it is all quite true.

ADEIMANTUS. Then how is it right to say that our states will never be free from their ills till the philosophers, who—you yourself say—are useless, become their rulers?

SOCRATES. Your question needs a comparison or parallel as an answer.

ADEIMANTUS. And you, I take it, aren't given to parallels!

SOCRATES. Are you laughing at me after driving me into (488) such a corner? Still, hear my parallel, you'll see then how forced it is. For so cruel is the condition of the better sort of philosopher in relation to the state that there is no one thing on earth which is quite like it. So, as a parallel for it, and an answer for them, one has to mix things together as the painters do in pictures of goat-stags and such animals. See then something of this sort taking place on a ship. Picture the pilot as taller and stronger than any of the others on this ship, but a little poor in his hearing and without the very sharpest eyes, and not much better at keeping his direction at sea. And let the sailors be in violent argument over who is to take the wheel, everyone saying it is his right, though he has never learned anything about that art and isn't able to point to any teacher or any time when he worked at it. And, what is more, they all say that there is no way of teaching it, and are ready to cut to bits anyone who says there is. And, all this time, they are hanging round the pilot, begging him to hand over the wheel and stopping at nothing to make him do so. And sometimes, if they don't manage it, and others get his ear, they put them to death or throw them overboard. Then, after putting the good pilot in chains or sending him to sleep with strong drink or making him unconscious somehow, they take over control of the ship, use up its stores, and so, drinking and having a great time, they make such a journey of it as might be looked for from such people. And as if that was not enough, they praise and cry up, as a fine seaman, a true sailor and a great pilot, the man who is cleverest in getting or forcing the true pilot to let them rule; while the man who isn't with them in this, they say is a good-for-nothing. They have no idea at all that a true pilot has to give his attention to the time of the year, the changes of the weather, the sky, the winds, the stars, and all the other things that come into his art, if he is to be a true ruler of a ship, and that he does not see how it is possible for there to be an art of no more than getting the wheel into one's hands with or without others' agreement, or how that would-be art is to be learned or united at the same time with the science of looking after the ship rightly. Won't such sailors say the (489) true pilot has his eyes on the stars only and is a useless do-nothing talker? You see the parallel, I take it. The best philosophers are of no use to the masses of men, but the cause of this is not in the best minds themselves, but in those who will not make any use of them.

ADEIMANTUS. You are very right.

SOCRATES. Under these conditions, philosophy, the highest way of life of all, will probably not be much respected by those whose ways are quite the opposite. But by far the greatest and chief damage to the name of philosophy is done by those who would have us believe they are philosophers. And now the thing to do is to see why most of them are rogues and why philosophy is not responsible for that.

ADEIMANTUS. Certainly.

SOCRATES. Let us go back to the good and gentle man (490) whose desire for the true is his guide. He naturally attempts, with all his heart, to get to true being; he will not rest with the things which opinion takes to be this or that, but will go on, with desire still sharp and strong, till he comes into touch with that in everything which makes it what it is, through that part of his mind whose business it is to mate with such true being—the part which is of like mind with it. Coming truly into connection with it, he will beget reason and what is true; and thus he will know and grow and truly live, and then and not till then rest from his labour.

ADEIMANTUS. The best possible account of it.

SOCRATES. But why are most so-called philosophers rogues? You will agree now that a true philosopher will be no common growth among men?

ADEIMANTUS. Most certainly.

SOCRATES. See how many and great are the forces which (491) work for his destruction. And the most surprising point of all is that every one of his praised natural powers tends to make its owner worse and turn him away from philosophy. I have in mind courage and temperance and the whole list.

ADEIMANTUS. That does sound strange.

SOCRATES. In addition all the things commonly named goods can destroy and turn away the mind: money, beauty and strength, powerful family connections, everything like that—you get my general sense here?

ADEIMANTUS. I do, but let me have a clearer statement of it.

SOCRATES. It is everywhere true of every seed and growth in animal or plant, that the more forceful it is the more it falls away from its right being when it does not get the food, rain, or place it needs. So the souls who are naturally ablest become worse than the others if their education goes wrong. Do great crimes and unmixed evil come from feeble souls or from strong ones, bent by bad training? A weak nature will never do anything great, for good or evil.

ADEIMANTUS. You are right.

SOCRATES. If the planting of the seed and its growth are under the wrong conditions, the outcome will be terrible (492)—unless some god helps. Or are you one of the people who believe it is Sophists who make young men go wrong? Are not the public who say such things themselves the greatest of all Sophists—training and forming after their own hearts young and old, men and women?

ADEIMANTUS. When do they do this?

SOCRATES. When the masses crowd together in public meetings, in the Assembly, at a trial, in the theatre or the camp, crying out, full-throated, that some of the things done are bad and others good, and clapping their hands till the very stones send their approval or ill will back as loud again. At such times, will not a young man's heart, as the saying is, be moved within him? What private teaching won't be washed away by such a river? Taken up by its current, he will say as they say, do as they do, and be as they are.

ADEIMANTUS. There is no help for it, Socrates.

SOCRATES. And moreover, we haven't yet pointed out the chief force at work.

ADEIMANTUS. What is it?

SOCRATES. What these trainers and Sophists, the public, back up their words with if their words haven't the desired effect: punishments, fines and loss of rights and death. What other Sophist or what private teaching will overcome that?

ADEIMANTUS. None.

SOCRATES. No, the very attempt would be foolish. As things are, if anyone anywhere comes to good, that must be through some sort of heavenly inspiration. For there is not, never has been, and never will be any keeping to true values and virtues for a soul which gets the opposite (493) education public meetings give. It is as if a man were learning the impulses and desires of some great strong beast, which he had in his keeping, how to come near it and touch it, and when and by what it may be made most violent or most gentle. Yes, and the cries it makes under which conditions, and what sounds from its keeper and others make it angry or quiet. And after getting this knowledge by living with the great beast long enough, he names it 'wisdom' and makes up a system and art, and gives that as his teaching—without any knowledge as to which of these opinions and desires is beautiful or ugly, good or bad, just or unjust. But he fixes all these words by the tastes of the great beast, and names what pleases it 'good', and the things which make it angry 'bad', having no other account to give of them. And what is necessary he names 'just' and 'high', never having seen how very different are *what must be* and *what should be*. So he is not able to make that clear to another. By heaven, won't such a man give the young a strange education? Have you ever heard an argument to the effect that whatever the public praises is good and beautiful, which wouldn't make you simply laugh?

ADEIMANTUS. No, and I am not looking for one.

SOCRATES. Never will the masses be a philosopher. But (494) they and all those who desire to keep in with them will say hard things of the philosophers.

ADEIMANTUS. Clearly.

SOCRATES. Then how is anyone who is naturally a philosopher from birth to be saved? Even as a boy among boys, he will take the first place, especially if his body matches his mind. His family and friends will desire, I take it, to make use of him, when he is older, for their own purposes. So they will make up to him with requests and rewards, to get into their hands now, by pleasing him, the power that will later be his.

ADEIMANTUS. That is what is done as a rule.

SOCRATES. What is a young man to do, if he is a citizen in a great state, of good family and well off, good-looking and tall? Won't his mind be full of unlimited high-flying hopes;

won't he see himself as able to manage all the business of the Greeks and the rest of the world, and with that in his head and no other solider ideas there, won't he be full of strange designs and senseless thoughts?

ADEIMANTUS. Undoubtedly, he will.

SOCRATES. And if to a man in this condition someone gently comes and says, which is true, that there is no sense in him and that he is badly in need of some, and that the only way to get some is to work like a slave for it, won't it be hard for him even to listen? And even if one young man does take something in and is moved by the attractions of philosophy, what will those others do as they see themselves having to give up his help and his company? Is there anything they will *not* do to keep him from such teaching, and to put away—by private designs or by public attack (495) before the judges—anyone who attempts it? Is it possible for such a man to live as a philosopher?

ADEIMANTUS. It is not.

SOCRATES. Then, because her rightful lords turn away, strange to themselves and untrue, philosophy, friendless and unwed, is attacked and shamed by evil-minded lovers, who give her the bad name you say she has and with some reason. For other little men, seeing this field open and full of fair names and high honours, jump joyfully out of their own trades into philosophy—those that are sharpest at their own little businesses. For in comparison with the other arts, the name of philosophy, even in her present low state, is still very much looked up to. And this is her attraction for those with feebler powers, whose souls are bent and crushed by their low interests, as their bodies are by their work. Aren't they just like some little bald tinker who has come into money and been let out, and had a bath and got himself up to be married to his master's (496) daughter, who is now poor and living by herself?

ADEIMANTUS. What a parallel!

SOCRATES. And what will the offspring be like? Won't it be false and low, nothing true or with any part in wisdom?

ADEIMANTUS. No doubt.

SOCRATES. For the rest there will be a handful of true disciples of philosophy—someone of good birth and training, maybe, who has been sent out of his country young, and so kept away from those who would make him untrue; or a great soul born in a little state may take no interest in its politics; or a small group who are right in turning away from lesser arts may come under her attraction; and some may be like our friend Theages—everything was taking him from philosophy into politics, but ill-health was the bridle which kept him safe—and for myself, the inner sign I have from the gods needs no word here, for it has been given to none or almost none before, I believe. And those who have been of this little company and have tasted how sweet and saving a thing philosophy is, have come to see, well enough, how far out of their minds the mass of men are, and that there is nobody who does anything straight or right in present governments, or any supporter of justice at whose side they may fight and be saved. A philosopher is like a man coming among violent beasts unwilling to take part in their ill-doings, and unable by himself to make head against them. He sees that long before he could do his friends or the state any good, he would come to an early end without having been useful to himself or to others. So, for all these reasons, the philosopher keeps quiet and minds his own business, like a man taking cover under a wall when clouds of ice and dust are driving by on the wind. Seeing others without any law or order in them, he is happy enough if he may keep himself free from injustice and ill-doings in this life and then gladly go away with a good hope, calm and peaceful when the end comes.

ADEIMANTUS. Well, that is not a little thing to have managed before he goes away.

SOCRATES. But not the greatest; *that* he won't do if he is (497) not living in a society which gives him the chance. Only in such a society will he come to his full growth, and save himself and the state as well. So now we have seen why men are against the philosophers.

ADEIMANTUS. No more on that, but which of our present-day forms of state is ready for him?

SOCRATES. None of them, which is what I have against them. The seed is overpowered and turned into another thing in such earth. But if there was ever a state which matched philosophy, then you would see how godlike she is; all the rest in man is manlike.

ADEIMANTUS. Would it be the state we were designing?

SOCRATES. In all respects but one: we would have to have some living authority in the state to keep in view the reasons why it was made so. And that authority would be philosophy, but it would have to be so managed that the philosophy was not the destruction of the state. But all great things are full of danger. 'Hard is the beautiful', as men say. See how brave my words are when I say that the state would have to treat philosophy in the very opposite way to our current doings.

ADEIMANTUS. How is that?

SOCRATES. At present, those who take up philosophy are (498–502) quite young, not more than boys. While waiting to go into business they have a shot at the hardest part of all—which is discussion, or dialectic—and then drop it. And these are thought to be the ones who have been most philosophic. Later they take themselves to be doing a great thing if, when requested, they give some attention to a philosophic discussion. That sort of thing isn't their business. When they are old, with most of them, out the light goes more completely than Heracleitus' sun, for *they* don't light up again!

ADEIMANTUS. Well, what is the right thing to do?

SOCRATES. The very opposite. When they are boys let them have an education and philosophy made for the young. While they are growing, let them take good care of their bodies to get a base and support for their use later by philosophy. Then with the growth of the soul, let the gymnastics of the mind be increased and, when their bodies become less strong and they are past the time of public and military work, then at last let them freely range in the fields of thought and do nothing seriously but philosophy. So may they be truly happy when the end comes and crown their days here with a like fate hereafter.

ADEIMANTUS. You seem deeply serious, Socrates, but most of your hearers are even more serious in taking the opposite view and you won't make them change it, Thrasymachus least of all.

SOCRATES. Don't try to set Thrasymachus and me against one another. We have just become friends. I'm not saying we were enemies before. Let me go on. Such philosophers won't be many, for these great powers don't (503) as a rule go together with being able to keep to ordered, quiet and peaceful ways of living; such men, because they are so quick, are driven every way by chance and all solid purpose goes out of them. And on the other hand, the men of solid purpose that one would more readily believe in, who in war are not lightly moved and are slow to fear, are unhappily much the same when faced with a book. They come into motion slowly; learning is hard for them as if they were numb, and when there is work for the mind to do, sleep attacks them and they are always yawning.

ADEIMANTUS. So it is.

SOCRATES. You have kept in mind that, after separating (504) the three forms in the soul, we gave our account of justice, temperance, courage, and wisdom?

ADEIMANTUS. If I hadn't I ought not to hear the rest!

SOCRATES. Well, we said then that, for the truest knowledge of these things, we would have to take a longer way, which would make them clear to the man who took it, but otherwise it would only be possible to give arguments like those which had gone before. And you said that would be enough for you. Was it?

ADEIMANTUS. Well, it was good measure for me, and the rest of the company seems satisfied.

SOCRATES. Not good measure, my friend, for nothing that falls short is the measure of anything, though some people are very ready to say that they have done enough and that there is no need to go farther.

ADEIMANTUS. Yes, they have that feeling because they hate trouble.

SOCRATES. A feeling least suited to the guardians of a state and its laws. A guardian will have to take the longer way and work as hard at learning as in gymnastics, or he won't ever come to this highest science, which is his true business.

ADEIMANTUS. What, aren't these things the greatest? Is there still something greater than justice and these other qualities?

SOCRATES. There is something greater. But we have to work these qualities themselves out to the last limit, not only look at an outline, as we have been doing. Wouldn't it be foolish to do everything to get our knowledge of unimportant little things as clear and right as possible and not attempt the same with the greatest things?

ADEIMANTUS. Certainly it would. But don't think we will let you go without saying what this greatest science is and what it works at!

SOCRATES. You have often heard the answer, but now, maybe, you don't see where I am going. Probably that is it. For you (505) have heard times enough that the greatest thing to learn is the idea of good, through which, only, just things and all the rest become useful and do good. And now I am almost certain you see that this is what I am going to talk about and that I am going to say, moreover, that we haven't enough knowledge of it. Even though we had ever so much knowledge of other things, that would do us no good. Would owning every other thing profit us if we didn't own anything good? Or any experience without experience of what is beautiful and good?

ADEIMANTUS. By Zeus, no!

SOCRATES. But most men believe pleasure is the good, and the ablest of them believe it is knowledge.

ADEIMANTUS. Certainly.

SOCRATES. And those who take this last view are not able to point out which knowledge it is, but in the end have to say it is knowledge of the good.

ADEIMANTUS. Foolish of them.

SOCRATES. Yes, they start by attacking us for not knowing the good and then turn round and talk as if we knew! And those who say good is pleasure are no less mixed in their wonderings than the others. Aren't they forced to say there are bad pleasures?

ADEIMANTUS. Most certainly.

SOCRATES. The outcome is that they say the same things are good and bad. And so the argument is endless. Again, isn't it clear that with the just and the beautiful there are numbers ready to *seem* just only, or to have what *seems* beautiful only, without its being so in fact; but with the good, everyone goes after the thing itself, and what only *seems* good is not good enough for anyone?

ADEIMANTUS. That is clear.

SOCRATES. This, then, every soul looks for, and for this every soul does all that it does, feeling in some way what it is, but troubled and uncertain and unable to see clearly enough. The soul forms no fixed belief about the good as it does about the other things. For that very reason, it does not get any possible profit there may be in those other things. And are the best men in our state, in whose hands everything (506) is to be placed, are they to be equally in the dark about something so important as this?

ADEIMANTUS. They least of all.

SOCRATES. The beautiful and the just will not have much of a guard in a man without that knowledge. No one will see what *they* are if he doesn't know what the good is. So only under a guardian who has this knowledge will our republic become perfectly ordered.

ADEIMANTUS. But you yourself, Socrates, do you think it is knowledge that is the good, or pleasure, or something different?

SOCRATES. There you are! Hearing what others say isn't enough for you.

ADEIMANTUS. But, Socrates, it does not seem right for you, after working at these questions so long, only to give the opinions of others.

SOCRATES. Well, does it seem right to you to talk as if one had knowledge, when one hasn't got it?

ADEIMANTUS. Not at all as having *knowledge*; no one has a right to do that; but you may say what your opinion is, as an opinion.

SOCRATES. But haven't you noted that opinions separated from knowledge are ugly things, blind, even the best of them? Are those who have some true opinion without reason very different from blind men who chance to go the right way? So is it these ugly things you would be looking at, bent eyeless things, when you might hear things beautiful and light-giving from others?

GLAUCON. Let me beg you, Socrates. Don't turn away now when you are so near. It will be enough for us if you do with the good what you have done with justice, temperance, and so on.

SOCRATES. It would be more than enough for me. No, my friend, let us put aside, for the present, the question of the true being of good; for to get to what is in my thoughts now about that seems to be an undertaking higher than the impulse which keeps me up today. But of what seems the offspring of the good, and most like it, I am willing to talk if so you desire. If not, we will let it drop.

GLAUCON. Go on and make the full payment—the account of its father—another time.

SOCRATES. I would that I were able to make, and you to (507) take, the full payment and not only the interest. But, at least, here is the interest, the offspring of the good. But be careful I don't mislead you with a false account of this interest.

GLAUCON. We will take care of that. Go on.

SOCRATES. Let us first agree on a point we have gone over before this.

GLAUCON. What is that?

SOCRATES. The old story, how we use the words 'to be' of numbers of beautiful things and good things, saying of them separately that *they are*. That's how we talk of them. And again we talk of a self-beautiful, and of the good in itself, and so with each of these things we then said were many; we talk of one thing, one Idea, which is that through which they are what they are.

GLAUCON. That is so.

SOCRATES. And the first sort of things we say may be seen but not thought, while thought but not sight may come to the ideas? Have you ever noted that sight was made with far more care than the other senses?

GLAUCON. Not specially.

SOCRATES. Look at it this way: do hearing and the voice need a go-between, without which the one won't hear and the other won't be heard?

GLAUCON. They don't need any such thing.

SOCRATES. And some of the other senses don't, though I'm not saying none of them do. But note that seeing and what is seen do need a go-between.

GLAUCON. How?

SOCRATES. Though the eye may have the power to see and its owner may attempt to use it, and though colour may be present, without a third thing specially made for the purpose, the power of seeing will see nothing and the colour won't be seen.

GLAUCON. What is this third thing you are talking about?

SOCRATES. The thing you name light.

GLAUCON. True.

SOCRATES. A great and high thing it is which yokes together (508) the powers to see and to be seen, nobler in form than anything the other senses have; and which of the gods of the sky will you name the maker and cause of light which makes vision beautifully see and things be seen?

GLAUCON. Why, the one you and all the others would name, for you are clearly talking about the sun.

SOCRATES. Isn't this the relation of vision to that god? Vision itself and that in which it lives, the eye, are not the sun.

GLAUCON. Certainly not.

SOCRATES. But the eye is, isn't it, the most like the sun of all the instruments of the senses? And doesn't it take in its power to see, as something that comes to it, from the sun?

GLAUCON. Yes.

SOCRATES. And is it not true again that, though the sun is not the power to see, it is the cause of that power and is itself seen by it?

GLAUCON. Yes, that is so.

SOCRATES. The sun, then, is what I named the offspring of the good which the good begot to be the parallel to itself. It was to be to seeing and the things which are seen, what the good is to thought and to what thought is of.

GLAUCON. How is that? Make it clearer.

SOCRATES. When sunlight isn't on things, but only the lights of the night, the eyes become unclear, they seem to have no power of seeing in them. But when there is sunlight on the things, they see clearly, and the seeing seems to be in the eyes.

GLAUCON. That is so.

SOCRATES. Take this as a parallel to the soul. When its attention is on whatever is bright with true being, the soul takes it in, and has deep knowledge of it and seems itself clearly to be full of thought and reason; but when it is turned to the twilight things which come and go, it forms opinions only, its edge is dulled, and first it has one and then another opinion as if it were without thought or reason. This, then, which gives true being to whatever deep knowledge is of, and the power to get this knowledge to whatever gets it, is to be named the idea of the good, and you are to see it as being the cause of knowledge, and of what is true in so far as there is knowledge of it. But beautiful though deep knowledge and the true are, you will be right in believing that there is something still more beautiful. And, as it was right before not to take seeing and (509) light to be the sun, though they are sunlike, so here you will take knowledge and the true to be their parallels and like the good, but don't take them to be the good. The good has a still higher place of honour.

GLAUCON. Beautiful beyond thought will it have to be, if it is that which gives us knowledge and the true and is still more beautiful than they are. You are certainly not saying that it is pleasure.

SOCRATES. Hush! But take a look at this parallel farther. The sun, wouldn't you say, not only gives a thing its power to be seen, but its generation and growth, though the sun is not itself generation? So too, you are to say, things are known only because the good is present; both what they are and that they are come from the good. But the good is not being, but is far higher in honour and power.

GLAUCON. Heavens! That out-tops everything!

SOCRATES. You forced me to say what my thoughts were about it.

GLAUCON. Don't stop. But do at least stretch out the parallel with the sun, if there is anything you are not giving us.

SOCRATES. Well, in fact, I am letting more than a little go.

GLAUCON. Don't let the least bit.

SOCRATES. I fear I'll have to, but, as far as I may, I won't willingly overlook anything. See then, there are these two, and one rules over the world of thought, the other over the field of what may be seen. Have you got these two sorts of things? Picture them in this way.

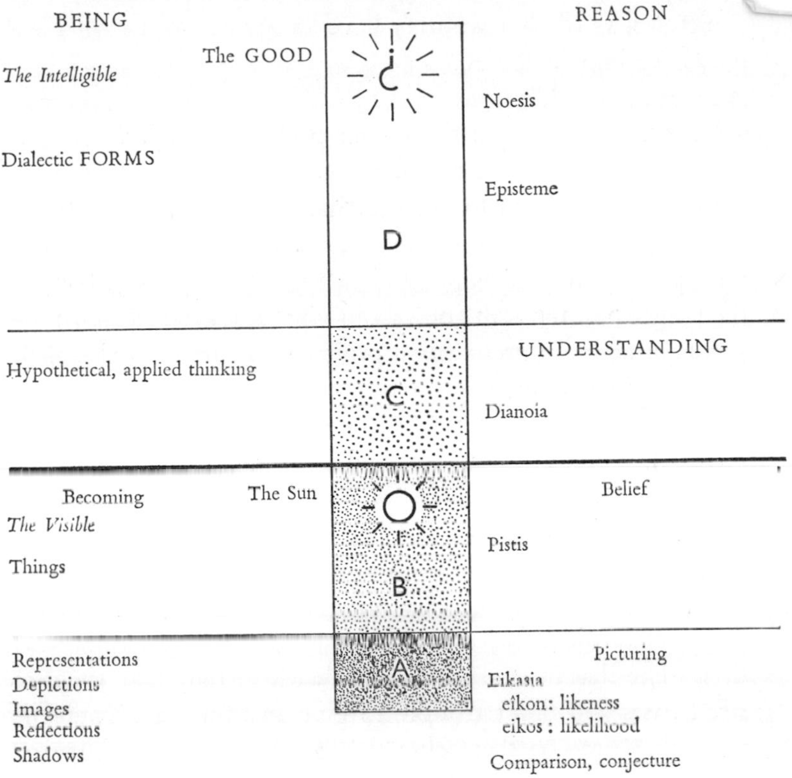

BEING

REASON

The Intelligible

The GOOD

Noesis

Dialectic FORMS

Episteme

D

Hypothetical, applied thinking

C

UNDERSTANDING

Dianoia

Becoming

The Visible

The Sun

Belief

Pistis

Things

B

Representations
Depictions
Images
Reflections
Shadows

A

Picturing

Eikasia
eîkon: likeness
eikos: likelihood

Comparison, conjecture

$$A : B :: A + B : C + D :: C : D$$

Take a line and cut it into two unequal parts—the short part for seeing, the long one for thought. Then cut those two parts again in the same unequal measure. Now these divisions will be representative of degrees of being clear. As the shorter part of what may be *seen*, come pictures: (510) first shadows, then images in water and in smooth, bright and polished things, glass and the like. In the longer part are all the things that these copying images are of—that is, the animals about us, plants, and all the things man makes.

GLAUCON. I see.

SOCRATES. Wouldn't you say, then, that as the picture is to what it pictures, so is what we may have an opinion of to what we may have knowledge of?

GLAUCON. I would.

SOCRATES. Now look at the longer part of the line, which has to do with *thought*. The soul, when it goes into the shorter part of this, is forced to take all that may be seen (the things pictured before) as themselves pictures, and from them it goes not up to the first principle, but down to an outcome. But in the longer part the soul goes, from what it takes as its starting-points, straight on up to a first principle of a higher order than these starting-points, and in this it uses no pictures of ideas, but through ideas alone makes its discovery of an ordered way.

GLAUCON. I don't fully understand all that.

SOCRATES. Let me make another attempt. You will understand better now that this has gone before. You know that in geometry, arithmetic, and so on, those who work at them simply take it that there are the even numbers and the not-even, the various triangles, circles, and such, three sorts of angles, and things like that in every branch of science; they take them as fixed bases and don't trouble to give any further account of what they are—to themselves or to others, simply believing that they are clear enough to everybody. They start out from these assumptions, and go on from them, in an ordered way, till they come to the end for which they started.

GLAUCON. Yes, that I do see.

SOCRATES. And, moreover, they make use of the things that may be seen and talk about them, though it is not *them* they have in mind, but the forms they represent. Their questions are about the square itself, *as such*, and the diagonal, *as such*, not about any one picture they make of it only. And so throughout. These very things—which have their shadows and images in water—they take as in their turn only copies, and what (511) they attempt to get at are their forms which are only to be seen by the mind.

GLAUCON. True.

SOCRATES. In this shorter division of the line we have to do with ideas, but with these two limits. First, that here the soul is forced to use bases or starting-points; it does not go on up to what they depend on, for it is unable to escape from and get up higher than these starting-point bases; secondly, that it uses, as mere pictures or parallels, the very physical things which are themselves pictured and paralleled by the images in the sort lower down still. And in comparison with these, they are said to be very clear and are given a high position.

GLAUCON. I see. You are still talking of what comes under geometry and the sister arts.

SOCRATES. And by the other, higher, division of thought you will see I mean that of which reasoning itself takes hold by the power of dialectic discussion. The things reasoning takes as bases are not taken by it as unquestioned starting-points, but as hypotheses, as helps or stepping-stones, as something to give a footing, or as springboards, by which it is made able to go up to that which is no such base which needs to be taken, but is that on which all depends. And after getting to that, it takes again a grip of the first things dependent on that, and goes down again to the outcome, making no use of any of the things of the senses but only of ideas themselves, moving on through ideas to ideas, and ending with ideas.

GLAUCON. I see, but not completely, for you seem to me to be talking of a very great undertaking; but I do see you are saying that the field of true being and thought, which is looked into by the science of dialectic discussion, is something clearer and more certain than the field of the arts, as they are named, whose starting-points are what *they* take as bases. And though, it is true, men in these arts have to work with their thought and not with their senses, still, because they don't go back to what all depends on, but simply use these bases, you do not think they are reasoning about them—though the bases themselves are things of reason when taken together with what makes them what they are. And you will give another name to what is done in geometry and the like, say understanding, not reason, because for you it is something in between opinion and reason.

SOCRATES. That account is quite good enough; and now, parallel to the four parts of our line, let us say there are four powers of the soul: Reason is the highest; Understanding the second; Belief the third; and Picturing is the last. Let us say that they are to one another as the things they have to do with are to one another, and that they are clear in the degree in which the things they have to do with have truth in them.

GLAUCON. I see. I'm in agreement with you, and I am ordering them as you say.

BOOK VII

SOCRATES. Now compare our condition with this: Picture (514) men living in a cave which has a wide mouth open towards the light. They are kept in the same places, looking forward only away from the mouth of the cave and unable to turn their heads, for their legs and necks have been fixed in chains from birth. A fire is burning higher up at their backs, and between it and the prisoners there is a road with a low wall built at its side, like the screen over which puppet players put up their puppets.

GLAUCON. All that I see.

SOCRATES. See again, then, men walking under cover of this low wall carrying past all sorts of things, copies of men (515) and animals, in stone or wood and other materials; some of them may be talking and others not.

GLAUCON. This is a strange sort of comparison and these are strange prisoners.

SOCRATES. They are like ourselves. They see nothing of themselves but their own shadows, or one another's, which the fire throws on the wall of the cave. And so too with the things carried past. If they were able to talk to one another, wouldn't they think that the names they used were those of the shadows that went by? And if their prison sent back an echo whenever one of those who went by said a word, what could they do but take it for the voice of the shadow?

GLAUCON. By Zeus, they would.

SOCRATES. The only real things for them would be the shadows of the puppets.

GLAUCON. Certainly.

SOCRATES. Now see how it will be if something frees them from their chains: When one is freed and forced to get on his feet and turn his head and walk and look towards the light—and all this hurts, and because the light is too bright, he isn't able to see the things whose shadows he saw before—what will he answer, if someone says that all he has seen till now was false and a trick, but that now he sees more truly? And if someone points out to him the things going by and asks him to name them, won't he be at a loss? And won't he take the shadows he saw before as more real than these things?

GLAUCON. Much more real.

SOCRATES. And if he were forced to look straight at the light itself, wouldn't he start back with pained eyes? And if someone pulled him up the rough and hard floor of the cave and (516) forced him out into the light of the sun, wouldn't he be angry? And wouldn't his eyes be too full of light to make out even one of the things we say are real?

GLAUCON. Yes, that would be so at first.

SOCRATES. He would need to get used to the light before he could see things up there. At first he would see shadows best, and after that reflections in still water of men and other things, and only later these things themselves. Then he would be ready to look at the moon and stars, and would see the sky by night better than the sun and the sun's light by day. At last, I take it, he'd be able to look upon the sun itself, and see it not through seemings and images of itself in water and away from its true place, but in its own field and as it truly is.

GLAUCON. So.

SOCRATES. And with that he will discover that it is the sun which gives the seasons and the years, and is the chief in the field of the things which are seen, and in some way the cause even of all the things he had been seeing before. If he now went back in his mind to where he was living before, and to what his brother slaves took to be wisdom there, wouldn't he be happy at the change and pity them?

GLAUCON. Certainly, he would.

SOCRATES. And if their way was to reward those who were quickest to make out the shadows as they went by and to note in memory which came before others as a rule, and which together, would he care very much about such rewards? And, if he were to go down again out of the sunlight into his old place, would not his eyes get suddenly full of the dark? And if there were to be a competition then with the prisoners who had never moved out and (517) he had to do his best in judging the shadows before his eyes got used to the dark—which needs more than a minute—wouldn't he be laughed at? Wouldn't they say he had come back from his time on high with his eyes in very bad condition so that there was no point in going up there? And if they were able to get their hands on the man who attempted to take their chains off and guide them up, wouldn't they put him to death?

GLAUCON. They certainly would!

SOCRATES. Take this comparison, dear Glaucon, with all we have said before: The world seen through the eyes, that is the prison house; the light of the fire is like the power of the sun; and if you take the way out, and that looking upon things of the upper world as the going up of the soul to the field of true thought, you will have my hopes or beliefs about it and they are what you desired—though only God knows if they are right. Be that as it may, what seems clear to me is that in the field of deep knowledge the last thing to be seen, and hardly seen, is the idea of the good. When we see it, we see that it is truly the cause, for all things, of all that is beautiful and right. In the world of visible things, it gives birth to light and to the lord of light, but in the field of thought it is itself the master cause of reason and all that is true; and anyone who is to act wisely in private or public must have seen this.

GLAUCON. I am with you—as far as I am able.

SOCRATES. It is not strange that those who have been so high are not willing to take up again the everyday business of men. Their souls are ever for turning again to that higher world. Nor, again, is it surprising if a man, coming back from such godlike visions to the evil condition of men, seems a poor and foolish thing in his behaviour; if before his eyes have got used to the dark again he is forced to go to law, for example, and fight about the shadows of justice or the images which make them, or argue about those images in the minds of men who have never seen justice itself.

GLAUCON. That isn't strange at all.

SOCRATES. Anyone who knew would keep in mind that (518) there are two ways in which the eyes may be troubled: when they change over from the light to the dark, and from the dark to the light. He'd believe that the same thing takes place with the soul, and he wouldn't be over-quick to laugh at a soul unable to see something, but would be careful to note if it were coming from a brighter light into the dark or were on its way from the deeper dark of little knowledge into daylight and if its eyes were unclear because the light was over-strong.

GLAUCON. A very just observation.

SOCRATES. If so, education is not truly what some of its professors say it is. They say they are able to put knowledge into a soul which hasn't got it—as if they were putting sight into blind eyes.

GLAUCON. They do say so.

SOCRATES. But our argument points to this: the natural power to learn lives in the soul and is like an eye which might not be turned from the dark to the light without a turning round of the whole body. The instrument of knowledge has to be turned round, and with it the whole soul, from the things of becoming to the things of being, till the soul is able, by degrees, to support the light of true being and can look at the brightest. And this, we say, is the good?

GLAUCON. We do.

SOCRATES. Of this very process, then, there might be an art, the art of turning the soul round most quickly, and with the most effect. It would not be an art of producing a power of seeing in the soul, for it has that already—though it has been looking in the wrong direction. It would be an art of turning the soul in the right direction.

GLAUCON. That seems probable.

SOCRATES. The other qualities of the soul do seem like those of the body, for even when they are not present from birth, they may be formed in it by training and use. But the quality of reason and thought, it seems, is a much more godlike thing whose power never goes away, but, as it is turned in one direction or another, becomes useful (519) and able to do good or useless and able only to damage. Haven't you noted, in those who are commonly said to be bad but sharp men, how quick their little souls are to see what is to their interest? It is clear they can see well enough. Only, the sharper their sight is, the worse are the things they do.

GLAUCON. Quite true.

SOCRATES. If from the earliest days this part of such a soul had been freed from the leadlike weights fixed to it at birth by the pleasures of taste and such, that now turn the soul's vision downwards; if, I say, the soul had been turned instead towards the things that are true and good, the same power in these same men would have been as quick to see the higher things as it is in seeing the low things it looks for now.

GLAUCON. Probably.

SOCRATES. And here is another thing which is probable, or, more truly, a necessary outcome of what we have said: those who are without education and true knowledge will never be able rulers of the state. And the same is true of those who never make an end of their education: the first because they have no one fixed purpose to give direction to all their acts, public and private; the others because they will not act at all, if they are not forced to, but believe they have been already transported to the Happy Isles. So we who are designing this state will have to force these naturally best minds to get what we have said is the greatest knowledge of all, to go on up till they see the good, and, when they have seen enough, we will not let them do as they do now.

GLAUCON. What is that?

SOCRATES. They may not keep to themselves up there, but have to go down again among those prisoners and take part in their work and rewards, whatever these may be.

GLAUCON. Then are we to wrong them by forcing them into a worse way of living when a better one is within their power?

SOCRATES. Are you keeping in mind, my friend, that this law of ours is not to make any one group in the state specially happy, but the state itself? Everyone is to give to (520) all the others whatever he is able to produce for the society. For it made these men so, not to please themselves, but to unite the commonwealth.

GLAUCON. I see. I was overlooking that.

SOCRATES. But note, Glaucon, there will be no wrong done to the philosophers in this. We have just arguments to give them when we force them to become guardians. We will say to them, 'It is natural that in other states men of your quality do not take part in the common work. For in these states such men come into being of their own sweet will and without the will of the government. Teachers of themselves, they have no cause to feel in debt to the state for an education they were never given. But you we begot to be rulers of yourselves and of the state. You have had a better and more complete education than any of the others; so down you go into the cave with the rest to get used to seeing in the dark. For then you will see far better than they do what these images are, and what they are of, for you have seen what the beautiful, the just and the good truly are.' So our state will be ruled by minds which are awake, and not as now by men in a dream fighting with one another over shadows and for the power and office which in their eyes are the great good. Truly that state is best and most quietly ruled where the rulers have least desire to be such, and the state with the opposite sort of rulers is the worst. And will you name any other sort (521) of man than a philosopher who looks down on political office?

GLAUCON. By Zeus, no.

SOCRATES. And now let us see how this sort of ruler is to be produced, and what sort of work will turn the mind from that which changes to that which is, turn it round from a day little better than night to the true daylight in the ascent we say is true philosophy.

GLAUCON. Certainly.

SOCRATES. Keep in mind that our guardians have to be ready for war. There were two parts in our education. Gymnastic had to do with the growth and decay of the body and so with coming to be and passing away. And that is not the sort of knowledge we are after. But what do you say of music which was, in a way, the (522) other part?

GLAUCON. Music was a parallel to gymnastic and trained the guardians through forming their ways of living, giving them harmony and rhythm, but no science. There was nothing leading to the sort of good you are looking for now.

SOCRATES. Your memory is right. There was nothing in music of that sort. But what branch of knowledge is there, dear Glaucon, of the sort we desire? For all the useful arts in our opinion are low.

GLAUCON. Undoubtedly. But if music and gymnastic are out, and the arts as well, what have we?

SOCRATES. We will have to take something which is not special but has to do with everything. Something which all arts and sciences and all forms of thought use. Something which everyone has to have among the first steps of this education.

GLAUCON. And what may that be?

SOCRATES. The simple business of knowing about one and two and three; in a word, number and arithmetic. Don't all the arts and sciences make use of them? Is not this the sort of science we are looking for, which naturally (523) takes us on into thought? But it has never been rightly used. Its true value is its attraction of thought towards being.

GLAUCON. Please make that clearer.

SOCRATES. Some accounts of things which the senses give us

do not make us think, for the senses seem good enough judges of them; but others do, because sense experience gives us nothing we may put any faith in.

GLAUCON. Clearly, what you have in mind is things seen at a distance or in paintings which trick the eye.

SOCRATES. No, that is not my point at all.

GLAUCON. Then what is it?

SOCRATES. The experiences which don't make us think are those in which the senses don't give opposite views. In those that do, I say, the sense, whatever the distance, no more gives us one thing than its opposite. An example will make this clearer: here are three fingers—the little finger, the second finger, and the middle finger.

GLAUCON. That is so.

SOCRATES. Every one of these seems equally to be a finger. Being seen as in the middle or at one side does not change that at all. Black or white, thick or thin, a finger is a finger all the same. For all these changes, the soul, in most men, is not forced to put any question like, 'What, then, is a finger?' For in seeing it, we are not at any point suddenly made to see that the finger is not a finger.

GLAUCON. Certainly not.

SOCRATES. Such an experience does not naturally make us think. But is this equally true of this point: are the fingers great or small? Will seeing answer that? And is that in no way changed by the fact that one of the fingers is in the middle and the others at the sides? And does touch, by itself, give us a good enough account of the qualities: thickness and thinness, softness and hardness? And so with the other senses. Do they give us good (524) enough accounts of such things? No, the soul needs something with which to judge them. And this is the knowledge of numbers. It is needed in the army, and a philosopher has to have it because he has to go up from out of the sea of becoming and take hold of being or he (525) will never use his reason rightly in arithmetic.

GLAUCON. It is so.

SOCRATES. So it is right, Glaucon, for this branch of learning to be ordered by law for those who are to take part in the highest work of the state. And they are to go into it till by the help of thought itself they come to see what numbers are. They are not to use it as the traders and the men in the market do, but for war and for the purpose of turning the soul itself away from becoming to being and the true.

GLAUCON. Well said. They are working with units (526) which are only to be taken up by thought and in no other way.

SOCRATES. Have you not noted how those who are naturally able at this science are generally quick in all others, and how men of slow minds, if they get nothing more from it, become sharper than they were before?

GLAUCON. That is so.

SOCRATES. And you will not readily name sciences which are more trouble to learn or to go on with than this. So for all these reasons let us keep this science in view and use it in the education of the naturally best minds.

GLAUCON. I am with you.

SOCRATES. With that point fixed, let us go on to the science which comes after this.

GLAUCON. What is that? Is it geometry?

SOCRATES. Yes.

GLAUCON. So much of it as is useful in war is certainly in place here. For an officer who was good at geometry would be very different from one who was not.

SOCRATES. But still, a very little geometry would be enough for that. What we have to see is if the greater and harder part of it farther on has a tendency to help us to (527–8) keep in view the idea of the good. But geometry itself is flatly against the language the experts in it use.

GLAUCON. In what way?

SOCRATES. They have no other way of talking than as if they were doing something with their hands and as if all their words had acts in view. For all their talk is of squaring or of putting one thing on top of another or of adding and the like. But in fact this science has nothing but knowledge itself in view—knowledge of that which always is and not of something which at one time comes into existence and then passes away.

GLAUCON. That we may agree about, for the knowledge of geometry is of what is always so.

SOCRATES. Then, my good friend, it will attract the soul towards the true, and will produce the philosophic way of thought, giving the powers which are now wrongly turned downward a direction upward.

GLAUCON. Nothing is more certain.

SOCRATES. Let us put this down as a second branch of knowledge for the men of your beautiful republic. And will astronomy be a third, or do you say 'No'?

GLAUCON. I am certainly with you, for quickness in noting the times of the year and the round of the months and years is very useful, not only in farming and at sea but still more in the military art.

SOCRATES. I am amused by the reason you give. You seem to fear that people may take you to be putting useless sciences forward. It is in fact very hard to see how in every soul there is an instrument of knowledge which may be cleared and put in order by such sciences when everyday business has broken and blinded it. And this instrument is of more value than ten thousand eyes, for by it only do we see what is true. Those who believe this with you will be very pleased with what we say. But those who have never had any experience of the sort will take us to be talking complete nonsense. For they don't see any profit to be got from such sciences. Make up your mind then, right away, which of them you are talking to.

GLAUCON. I see now I was wrong; and in place of that common sort of praise for astronomy, Socrates, let me say (529) this about it from your point of view. It will be clear to everyone that astronomy makes the soul look upward and takes it up from things here to higher things.

SOCRATES. It may be clear to everyone but me, for that's not what I think.

GLAUCON. Well, what do you think then?

SOCRATES. I think the astronomy men offer us today turns the mind's eye very much downward.

GLAUCON. How so?

SOCRATES. You seem to me to have a very wide view of this knowledge of higher things. For to you, it seems, a man with his head back looking up at ornaments on the ceiling would be using his higher reason and not his eyes. Maybe you are right and I am over-simple. But to me no true science which doesn't turn us toward being and the unseen makes the soul look upward. If anyone attempts to learn through the senses —whether by looking up at the sky or blinking at the ground— I would never say he was truly learning, for nothing of that sort is what science has to do with. His soul is looking down, not up—however much you stretch him on his back on the earth or in the sea!

GLAUCON. It was coming to me! But what *is* the right way of teaching astronomy?

SOCRATES. Like this: These ornaments of the sky are doubtless the most completely ordered of all visible things, but as such they are far short of what is true—their true motions, namely, their true number and forms in relation to one another. Men may get at these things by reasoning and the work of thought, but not by sight. Or have you a different opinion?

GLAUCON. Not at all. But you are giving men a thousand (530) times as much work as our present astronomers have in mind.

SOCRATES. Yes, and it will be the same with the other sciences if we are to be any use as law-makers. In all of (531) them, when we have gone far enough to see their connections and relations, and their togetherness, then all this work will point to our desired end, and the work itself will not have been wasted. But if we do not get so far it will be no use at all.

GLAUCON. It seems so to me as well; but, Socrates, this is a very great stretch of work you are talking of.

SOCRATES. Which is? This opening part or what? Don't you see that this is only the part that comes before the law itself, that true music which we have to learn? You certainly don't take the experts in these sciences to be good at discussion and dialectic?

GLAUCON. No, by Zeus. At least only a few of them in my experience.

SOCRATES. Will men who are unable to give and audit a full account of what may be meant in a discussion ever (532) know what we say must be known?

GLAUCON. 'No' is the answer to that as well.

SOCRATES. This then, at last, Glaucon, is the law itself, the true music played by dialectic. It is the work of thought, but has its parallel in our power to see—which, in my parallel or parable, comes after a time to see living things, and then the stars, and at last the sun itself. So it is with dialectic: when a man—through thinking about what we mean, putting the records of the senses on one side—attempts to make his way into the very being of each thing and keeps on till by thought itself he takes in what the good is itself, he comes to the limit of the world of thought, as the other in our parallel came to the end of what may be seen.

GLAUCON. Certainly.

SOCRATES. And this movement of thought you will name 'dialectic'.

GLAUCON. I will.

SOCRATES. And the freeing from the chains and the turning away from the shadows to the images, and to the light, and the going up from that dark cave under earth to the sunlight, and that increase of power to see real things in place of reflections merely and shadows thrown by a fire which was but an image of the sun—all that is the parallel to what these arts we have been talking of do for us, to their power to guide what is best in the soul up to the stage of looking up to what is best in the things which truly are—as in our parallel what is clearest in the body was turned round to see what is brightest of the bodily things which may be seen.

GLAUCON. I am with you and take this to be true. But it seems to me very hard to believe, though in another way it is hard not to believe it. Still, as we are not going to hear it this once only, but will be talking it over again and again, let us take these things to be true and go on now to the music of dialectic itself, and go through with it as we have gone through the opening part. So tell me what this dialectic power is? What are its divisions and what are its ways? For these would, it seems, take us to the place where we may rest from the road and come to the end of our journey.

SOCRATES. My dear Glaucon, you will not be able to (533) come farther with me, however willing I might be. If I were able, I would give you no longer any comparison, parable or picture, but the truth itself, as I see it, though if rightly or not is not for me to say. But that it is something like this we have to see, we may be certain. Is it not so?

GLAUCON. It is.

SOCRATES. And may we not say as well that nothing less than the power of dialectic itself will make this clear, and then only to a man experienced in these sciences we have been going over, and that this thing is not possible in any other way?

GLAUCON. We may be as certain of that.

SOCRATES. At all events, there will be no argument over this: there is no other way than dialectic through which we may by a regular process come to see what everything, in itself and in its true being, is. All the other arts have to do with men's desires and opinions, or with the growth and passing away of things, or with taking care of such things. And as for those which, we have been saying, are in some degree about true being—geometry and the sciences which go with it—they are, as it were, dreaming of this. They will not see with eyes fully awake while the bases they take off from are unchanged and while they are unable to give any account of them. For when what it all depends on is something which the reasoner does not know, and the end and everything that comes between are put together out of things he can't account for, how can any amount of *saying*, 'It is so!' be turned into true knowledge or science?

GLAUCON. It is not possible.

SOCRATES. The dialectic process, and that only, goes forward in this way, seeing through everything which may be taken as a fixed base to get to what it can really depend on and find its support there. The eye of the soul is in fact bedded deep in the wet soft earth of the Orphic story, and dialectic gently takes it out of this and guides it up—helped by the arts we were listing in this work of turning it round. We named these arts, sciences, as men generally do, but in fact they need some other name, as things clearer than opinion but not so clear as true science. 'Understanding', I believe, was the name we used. But I take it we will not be troubled about the name when more important things are before us to be looked into.

GLAUCON. No, truly.

SOCRATES. So it will be enough, maybe, to give the name *reason* to the first and highest division, to the second, *understanding*, (534) to the third, *belief*, and to the fourth, *picturing*. And the last two together we will name *opinion*, and the first two together will be *knowledge*. Opinion has to do with becoming and knowledge with true being. And we may put the relation between them like this: as being is to becoming, so knowledge is to opinion; and as knowledge is to opinion, so reason is to belief, and understanding to picturing. But the relations between what these four have to do with and the division of them separately into two parts—that which opinion is of, namely, and that which knowledge is of—let us put that on one side, Glaucon, or it will take us into a discussion far longer than that we have got through.

GLAUCON. Well, I'm with you about the rest of it as far as I am able to see it.

SOCRATES. And you will give the name dialectician to the man who is able to audit the account of the true being of each thing? And say that a man who is unable to do this, in so far as he is not able to make out such an account for himself or for others, has not the full use of reason there?

GLAUCON. Certainly I will.

SOCRATES. And is this not true as well of the good? If a man is not able to mark off in discussion and separate out from all other things the idea of the good, and take it through all the tests, looking always to what anything *is* and not to opinion about it, and go on through all this without a slip in his reasoning—if a man is without the power to do this, won't you say he hasn't a true knowledge of the good itself, or of any other good? Any shadow he grasps at is his through opinion, not through knowledge. Sleeping and half sleeping through all his days, before he is awake he will come to the house of Hades and there sleep on forever.

GLAUCON. Yes, by Zeus. I will say all that.

SOCRATES. We come then to the question of distribution. (535–6) Who are the persons to be put to this work and how? Take your mind back to the virtues we said our rulers were to have. He who would be a philosopher must not be half-hearted in his love of work. And if we let in any but the best in all ways, we will let loose a river of shame on philosophy. And keep in mind that at the start we made the rulers old men, but in this work that will not do. For we may not take Solon's word for it that an old man is able to learn much. He is no better at learning things than at running. No, all long and hard work is for the young.

GLAUCON. Necessarily.

SOCRATES. All these arts, geometry and the like, which are to make them ready for dialectic, are to be given to them while still young then, but not forced upon them.

GLAUCON. Why not?

SOCRATES. Because a free soul should not work like a slave. Forced bodily work does no damage to the body, but nothing learned through force from without takes root rightly in the mind. So, my friend, don't keep the young at their work by force but by play, and then you will see (537) better what their natural powers are.

GLAUCON. There is reason in that.

SOCRATES. And let those whose powers in all ways are greatest be put on a list.

GLAUCON. At what age?

SOCRATES. When they are through their gymnastics, for while they are doing that they won't be able to work with their minds. Being tired and oversleeping are no help in learning. But their behaviour in gymnastics will be one of our chief tests. After this, those who are on the short list of the twenty-year-olds will be given a special position and then they will have to take the arts and sciences they have been working at separately and put them into connection in a complete view of their relations with one another and with what truly is.

GLAUCON. Yes, that is the only sort of learning which stays with those who take it in.

SOCRATES. And it is, moreover, the chief test of the dialectic mind and its opposite. For he who is able to see all things in their connections with one another is a dialectician; he who is unable is not.

GLAUCON. I am in agreement.

SOCRATES. Then you will have to judge and see who come through best, who keep on best in their work and in war and in all the other things which the law puts them to, and when they are past thirty you will make another selection from your short list and give these a higher position still, and test them again by the help of dialectic to see which of them is able to give up the support of his eyes and other senses and go on, in company with all that is true, to being itself. And at this point, my friend, the greatest care is needed.

GLAUCON. Why specially here?

SOCRATES. Have you not noted how great is the damage done by our present ways with dialectic?

GLAUCON. What is that?

SOCRATES. Those who go in for it are lawless.

GLAUCON. They certainly are.

SOCRATES. Is there anything surprising about this, isn't it natural enough?

GLAUCON. Why is it so natural?

SOCRATES. As a parallel, picture to yourself a boy living (538) in a great and wealthy family, with wide and important connections, in which he believes he is a son. Round him are any number of smooth talkers who give him a very high opinion of himself. Now let him suddenly discover that he is not the son of those he took to be his father and mother, and his true father and mother no one is able to name. What, then, will be his behaviour towards these smooth-tongued ones and towards those he falsely took to be his father and mother? Will it be different before and after this discovery?

GLAUCON. Please say what *you* think.

SOCRATES. As I see it, so long as he is without knowledge of the fact, he will be respectful to his father and mother and to his other relations, as he takes them to be; more respectful than to those smooth talkers. He will give his attention to them before the others and take care of them and not go against their will in word or act. He'll do what they say in all important ways.

GLAUCON. Probably.

SOCRATES. But after his discovery, what then? Won't his respect and attention step by step go over to those who say pleasing things to him? Won't he take their suggestions more readily than before, measure things by their opinions, take up their ways, keep company openly with them? And if he isn't very good by birth, he won't in time trouble himself any more about those he took to be his relations.

GLAUCON. That is all very probable. But where is the parallel with our young dialecticians?

SOCRATES. Here. We have, haven't we, certain fixed opinions about what is just and beautiful? We have been trained up in them from our first days. They have been like father and mother to us, and we do what they say and respect them.

GLAUCON. Yes.

SOCRATES. And are there not other beliefs and ways of living different from these, which talk smoothly to our souls and offer them pleasures? But those attractions do not move men with a sense of measure. Such men respect the teaching of their fathers and keep to it.

GLAUCON. That is so.

SOCRATES. Well then, the question, 'What *is* to be respected?' comes up before such a man. He gives the answer which he learned from the lawgivers. But the argument makes him out to be wrong. And this takes place again and again in all sorts of ways, till he is forced to believe that nothing is any more to be respected than it is to be looked down upon, and he comes to the same opinion about the just and the good and the things he honoured most. What will he do then and what view will he have of these rules of the ways of living?

GLAUCON. He can't go on respecting them as before.

SOCRATES. And then, when he no longer sees them as having any force, and does not discover any true rule, (539) how will he keep from the ways of living which most please his desires?

GLAUCON. He will not.

SOCRATES. So you will have to take great care about how you turn your thirty-year-olds on to dialectic. And one chief thing which will make them safer is not to let them taste it while young. You have seen, haven't you, how boys, when they first taste the pleasures of argument, make a sport out of it, always using it to get the better of others? They copy those who out-argue them and out-argue others in their turn, and take endless pleasure like young dogs in pushing about and pulling to bits with words all who come near them.

GLAUCON. Yes, endlessly.

SOCRATES. And when they have overcome others and been overcome time and again, they quickly drop into a violent disbelief in all they before believed. And the outcome is that they themselves and all the business of philosophy get a very bad name with the rest of men.

GLAUCON. Most true.

SOCRATES. But an older man will not go out of his mind in this way. He will copy those who use dialectic to see what is true, not those who use it as a sport and in the war of words. He will be more measured and temperate, and so through him dialectic is more respected, not less.

GLAUCON. You are right.

SOCRATES. All our earlier statements had this in view: that those who are to take part in such discussions will have to have well-ordered and unshakable minds. We won't let any and every chance person come into this field.

GLAUCON. Certainly not.

SOCRATES. Our dialectician will give himself up to it without doing anything else, as he gave himself up to his gymnastics for let us say five years. After that you will have to send them down into the cave again, and force them to take any military or other office which is fitted for young men, so that they won't have less experience than other men. And in these positions they will (540) be tested again, to see if they are strong against every sort of temptation, or if they give way in anything.

GLAUCON. How long is this stage to be?

SOCRATES. Fifteen years. And when they are fifty those who have come through and are seen to be altogether the best in all their acts and in every branch of science are to come at last to that for which all this was to make them ready. They will have to turn upward the eyes of their soul and look up to that which gives light to all, and when in this way they have seen the good itself, let them use it as their example in the right ordering of the state, the citizens, and themselves. They will give the greater part of their time to philosophy, but when their turn comes they will work as servants of the state, taking office for the good of the state and looking on this not as something to be desired but as necessary. And so, when they have given those who are to take their place as guardians an education like their own, let them go to the Islands of the Blest. And the state will keep their memory green with offerings, as though to gods, if Apollo's oracle at Delphi lets it be so; if not we will think of them as blessed and godlike men.

GLAUCON. A most beautiful finish you have put on your men, Socrates, as though *you* were a maker of statues.

SOCRATES. And on the women too, Glaucon: don't take me to be talking of the men more than of those women who have the needed qualities.

GLAUCON. That is right; all is to be equally in common.

SOCRATES. Haven't we said enough now about this state (541) and about the sort of man who is its parallel, for what he will have to be is clear?

GLAUCON. It is, and nothing more needs to be said.

BOOK VIII

GLAUCON. Such, then, is the good constitution, and (543–4) such the good man; all the rest are bad and wrong—the societies and the parallel men. You said some time ago that there are four wrong forms. Which are they?

SOCRATES. The other forms of government—those for which we have special names—are these: First we have the spirited constitution as in Crete and Sparta, and the general voice is for it. Second in common opinion comes rule by a few, oligarchy, as its name is (or let us say plutocracy), and it is full of evils. Next, its enemy democracy. And last, that noble thing, tyranny, fourth and last disease of a state. Is there any other chief sort? Aren't the rest only different in details?

The number of different sorts of governments and of souls among men must be the same. For governments don't spring up out of stones and trees but from the quality of mind and way of living of the citizens—as the scale is turned by this or by that, and all the rest is (545) changed with it. Now let us see how aristocracy, rule by the best, the lovers of knowledge, turns into rule by lovers of honour. May we not take it as the rule for all these changes in governments, that they start *in* the ruling body and only when that body becomes the seat of divisions? While it is of one mind there is no way of (546–7) shaking it, even though it is small in numbers. And how does division start in our happy state? From the mixing of the men of iron and brass with the men of silver and gold. The iron and brass men tend to money-making and owning property. The better sorts give in to them and, in time, after a distribution of the land and houses among themselves, they make those they were guarding as free friends before into slaves and servants. And these rulers now take to making endless wars and keeping watch over the citizens.

GLAUCON. That is the way the change starts.

SOCRATES. What will this state be like after the change? In much it will copy our earlier aristocracy. But fear of putting really able men in office, because it no longer has any simple and serious men of that sort, but only mixed men and a tendency to respect too much men of spirit with (548) the narrower military virtues, will be its special marks. And its chiefs, like the plutocrats who will come later, have a great love of gold and silver, owning storehouses and private strong places in which to put them, and they will have walled-in houses, private love nests in which to use money with a free hand on women or any others they may please with it. Other men's money, that is, for they will take great care of their own, keeping it secret; and secret will they be in their pleasures as well, running away from the law like boys running from their father because they have not been trained by reason but by force.

GLAUCON. Certainly this constitution is very mixed.

SOCRATES. It is both good and bad; but because spirit takes such a high place in it, one thing will stand out—a love of taking sides and of being looked up to. That is the general outline. There is no need for details, which might be endless. Now what sort of man answers to this constitution and how does he come into being?

ADEIMANTUS. If he loves to take sides, he will be markedly like Glaucon, here!

SOCRATES. Maybe, but, in some of the points I am going on to, he is not so like Glaucon.

ADEIMANTUS. Which are they?

SOCRATES. He is more self-willed than Glaucon and cares less for the arts. Unlike a man with a better education (549) who looks down on slaves, he will be hard on them while he is naturally gentle to free men. He's very quick to please officials and loves high position and authority, which, he says, is rightly his, not as an orator or anything of that sort, but because he is a good fighter, being a man with a taste for gymnastics and field sports.

ADEIMANTUS. I see; that *is* the spirit of the society answering to him.

SOCRATES. In his younger days such a man is against wealth; but as he gets older he likes it better, for money-loving is part of his nature. He is generally the son of a very good father, who, since the state has a bad government, keeps clear of politics and high position, and lawsuits and all other chances for a quick and moving spirit, and is readier to lose some of his rights than to get into trouble. The son's spirited quality comes from the time when he first listens to his mother, who says she is looked down upon by the other women because her man is not in the government, isn't interested in money, and won't go to law or make a noise at the public meetings—to all of which things his father gives little attention. She notes that her husband is deep in thought all the time, and that he has no great opinion of her, though he is never without respect. For all of which reasons she is angry and is always saying to her son that his father is no man, but a good for nothing, not to add here all the words which women use in such connections.

ADEIMANTUS. Yes, they seem to have plenty to say.

SOCRATES. And, as you know, the servants in such houses—servants who seem to have the family's interest at heart—sometimes privately make somewhat the same observations to the son; and if they see a man in debt to the father, or troubling him in any other way, and the father does not go to law about it, they say to the son that when he is older, he will have to see to all this and be more of a man than his father. And he comes across (550) other examples of the same thing. He sees that quiet men who don't make trouble at public meetings are said to be simple while those who are always putting their fingers in other men's business are well thought of. On the other hand, he learns something about reason from his father and is pulled in two directions. In the end he takes a middle line and hands the government of himself over to the spirited part of his soul, and the outcome is a proud, honour-loving sort of man.

ADEIMANTUS. That's right.

SOCRATES. So we have the second constitution and the second man. Now may we go on to plutocracy and the parallel sort of man?

ADEIMANTUS. What sort of constitution is this?

SOCRATES. It is based on property. The wealthy rule and the poor have no part in the government. A blind man can see how this comes about. It's the gold in those private storehouses which puts an end to the spirited constitution. First the wealthy discover new ways of using their money, and little they care—they or their wives—about the law. Then they go in for competitive spending and thus the same stamp is put on the general body. And the farther they go down the money-getting road, the less is their respect for the true values. For are not money and virtue like the two scales of a balance: as one goes up the other (551) goes down?

ADEIMANTUS. That is quite true.

SOCRATES. Then they make a law, which is the mark of a plutocracy, by which no man without a certain amount of property may have any part in the government. And they take up arms to put this measure through if they have not been able to do it already through fear. Isn't that how it is done?

ADEIMANTUS. It is; but what chiefly is wrong with plutocracy?

SOCRATES. First, this very law; what if no man could be a pilot if he hadn't a certain amount of property? What if we kept a poor man out of that position though he was the better pilot?

ADEIMANTUS. We'd make sad work of the journey, so.

SOCRATES. Isn't this true of managing anything whatever?

ADEIMANTUS. Yes, as I see it.

SOCRATES. Anything but a state. Is that it?

ADEIMANTUS. A state more than any other thing; ruling *that* is the hardest and the most important work of all.

SOCRATES. And is this any better—that a plutocratic state

becomes not one but two: one state of the wealthy and another of the poor?

ADEIMANTUS. No, that is quite as bad.

SOCRATES. Again, it's certainly not a good thing to be—as they probably will be—unable to make war if the need comes? For if they put arms in the hands of the masses they will be more in fear of them than of those they are fighting. But if they don't make use of the masses, well, they'll seem oligarchs in more than name few enough when it comes to the test. Moreover, their love of money will make them very unready to give it up for the common (552) cause. But the worst thing of all about this sort of state is the number of unemployed it produces—people living in the state without having any place or position in it, men who are neither traders nor workmen nor soldiers, but without work of any sort or money either.

ADEIMANTUS. No other government so far lets anything of that sort take place.

SOCRATES. But here some of the citizens have too much money and others have lost everything. Those with too much, though they spend and spend to look as if they were in the ruling class, are doing nothing. They are of no use at all to the state, but only waste its goods. They are like drones in the hive, only a weight on the others, the workers. And though, Adeimantus, God doesn't give any of the flying drones stings, he has made only *some* of these walking drones stingless; some he has given stings enough to put fear into anyone. And while the drones without stings end up as beggars, the stinging drones are those from whom most of our crimes come. Whenever you see beggars in a society you may be certain that there will be crimes of all sorts as well.

ADEIMANTUS. True.

SOCRATES. Well, aren't there any number of beggars in plutocratic states?

ADEIMANTUS. Yes, almost all are beggars except the ruling class.

SOCRATES. So much for a plutocratic state. Now let us (553) take a look at the parallel man and how *he* is produced. That honour-loving man has a son, who at first takes after his father. Then suddenly he sees him being crushed by the government, his property and his person in danger together, sees him, after being at the head of his country's armies, or having held some other high post, taken before the judges under false charges, and maybe put to death or sent out of the country, or his rights as a citizen are taken away and all his property with them.

ADEIMANTUS. That might very well be true.

SOCRATES. Well, my friend, when the son sees all this, fear comes into his heart and pushes out what is spirited in him and loves honour. So he gives himself up to money-making, and, little by little, by putting small sums on one side and working hard, he becomes wealthy. Desire for profit rules like the Great King in him, and reason and spirit become its slaves, the one thinking of nothing but how to make money into more money, the other honouring nothing but property and men of property. Let's see now how this money-loving man is like the plutocratic (554) constitution. First, he puts wealth above everything. Second, he is careful and hard-working, and only gives himself what is necessary, keeping his other desires unemployed. In fact, he is the sort of man the vulgar admire.

ADEIMANTUS. Yes, property *is* what they most respect.

SOCRATES. Very true. And isn't he full of dronelike desires, some of them beggars and some of them criminals kept down in him only by his care for his own profit—he has no education to keep them in order. And to see the ill-doings which come from this, watch what he does to orphans when there is nothing to stop him. And when he does seem just, that is through fear, too—if he didn't his property might be in danger. And so such a person, far from being at peace with himself, will be a man of two minds, not of one mind—though generally his better desires will have the upper hand over the worse.

He will seem better from the outside than others; but the true virtue of a soul in agreement and harmony with itself he will not have.

ADEIMANTUS. Quite so.

SOCRATES. And now to the democratic state and the (555) parallel democratic man. Isn't the change from plutocracy to democracy produced by the same limitless desire for wealth, which is taken to be the greatest good? The rulers get their power from their wealth and are not very ready to stop young men from wasting their substance. They lend them money on their property and not infrequently take all that they have; so there they are, these men—armed, in debt, hating the new owners of their property, and working against them and against anyone better off than themselves. All such men are burning for revolution.

ADEIMANTUS. True.

SOCRATES. But the money-makers keep their eyes down and even make believe they don't see them; and whenever one of the rest gives them the chance, they poison him again with their credit, getting more back, in interest, (556) than they lent him, and making more drones and beggars for the state.

ADEIMANTUS. Yes, that they do.

SOCRATES. And they won't put an end to this great evil—either by not letting men do as they like with their property, or by ruling that such agreements are at the risk of those who go into them and debts may not be collected by force. If this were done, men would have more shame and take more care about giving credits, and the evils we are talking of would be less common in the state.

ADEIMANTUS. Much less common.

SOCRATES. As it is, the ruling class does all this and they themselves and their sons become soft and unwilling to work with body or soul and weak before pleasure and pain. And when rulers and ruled meet one another on some journey, say at sea, or in some hour of danger, and see one another's behaviour at such times, the poor aren't in fact a bit looked down on by the rich. When some wiry, sunburned, poor man finds himself next to some white-faced rich man, fat, breathless and helpless, when, I say, such things take place, is it possible for these poor men not to see that it is through the fears of the poor that such men have everything? How will they *not* say to one another when they meet in private, 'Our leaders are not much use!'

ADEIMANTUS. I'm quite certain they do say so.

SOCRATES. Now, in an unhealthy body a small push from without is all that is needed to make it ill. So with (557) this diseased state. And sometimes, even without a push from without, such a state goes to war within itself.

ADEIMANTUS. It does.

SOCRATES. Democracy then comes when the poor get the power, putting some who are against them to death, sending others away, and then letting everyone have an equal part in the rulers' rights and offices. And most commonly in such governments the positions are given by lot.

ADEIMANTUS. Yes, that is how a democracy comes into being, by force of arms or by the plutocrats giving up through fear.

SOCRATES. And now, what is such a constitution like? For clearly the democratic man will have to be marked by the same things. First, are they not *free* people? Doesn't the state become full of free acts and words; may not every man in it do whatever he will?

ADEIMANTUS. Yes, so they say.

SOCRATES. And clearly, when all men are so free, every citizen will take up whatever way of living pleases him.

ADEIMANTUS. He will.

SOCRATES. In this society there will be all sorts of different ways of living. So, possibly, this constitution may be the most beautiful of all? Ornamented with every sort of quality, it may be thought as beautiful as a dress ornamented with every sort of flower. And, maybe, as the young and as women have a taste for dresses with numbers of colours in them, so this sort of society will be thought the most beautiful.

ADEIMANTUS. No doubt it often will be.

SOCRATES. Yes, my friend, and if we were looking for new constitutions it would be a good idea to go into such a democracy with care.

ADEIMANTUS. Why?

SOCRATES. Because it has every sort of constitution in it—being so free. And maybe a person inventing a state, as we were, would do well to go through a democracy, as a sort of market of constitutions, and take the one which pleases him best, and build from it.

ADEIMANTUS. He won't be at a loss for different patterns.

SOCRATES. Again, in this state, you are not forced to take office, though you are quite able to do the work; and there is no need for you to do what the government says you are to do, if it is not your pleasure; or go to war, when the other citizens are at war; or keep peace when they are keeping peace, if that's not your desire; or again though a law says you are not to take office, or join the judges, you may none the less do both, (558) if the idea comes into your head. Now say if such a way of living is not godlike and full of pleasure, for the time being?

ADEIMANTUS. Maybe it is, for the time being!

SOCRATES. Again, is not the behaviour of some of the criminals in good taste? Have you not seen how, in such a republic, men who have been sentenced to death or sent away out of the country or put in prison are still there all the same, walking about the streets, like spirits, as if no one saw or cared a bit about it?

ADEIMANTUS. I have seen enough examples.

SOCRATES. What about the way such a government keeps its hands off them? How noble! Such things are not high enough to be noted by it. No. In fact it has a very poor opinion of the principle we were making so much of—that no one will ever become good, if, from his earliest days, he hasn't been playing among and giving his attention to good and beautiful things. How great-mindedly it puts all this underfoot, without troubling itself in the least about what the man who goes into politics has been doing before that—if only he says he loves the people.

ADEIMANTUS. Yes, it's all very noble!

SOCRATES. These, then, are some of the marks of a democracy, with which we might put others of the same family; and it will be, probably, a republic full of pleasure and different colours, but without law—doing the same on an equal footing to equals and to unequals.

ADEIMANTUS. Well enough we know it.

SOCRATES. Now, what about the man who is the parallel to democracy? Our careful plutocratic man has a son.

ADEIMANTUS. Why not?

SOCRATES. And this son, like his father, at first controls by force those desires in himself which don't make money but use it up. They are the unnecessary pleasures. (559) In our account of the 'drone' didn't we say he produced and was ruled by numbers of these unnecessary desires, while the plutocratic man was ruled by the necessary desires?

ADEIMANTUS. That is so.

SOCRATES. Now for the change over. It comes with this man's first taste of the honey of the drones, when he first makes friends with a number of violent beings within him who are able to get for him all sorts of strange pleasures. And these desires fight with the careful plutocratic ones, and sometimes they lose, and some (560) of them are destroyed or forced out, because there is still some sense of shame in the young man's mind; and order comes back again.

ADEIMANTUS. Sometimes.

SOCRATES. But sometimes, again, new desires of the same family are secretly nursed up, and because there was no wisdom in the education his father gave him they grow strong. And these desires, naturally, take him back to his old company and by their secret meetings numbers of other desires arise in him. And at last, seeing there is no knowledge there to guard it, they force their way into the very keep of the young man's soul. So he goes back to those *lotus-eaters*, living now with them openly and without making any secret of it. From that day on, (561) a man of this sort, I take it, gives quite as much money and work and time to unnecessary as to necessary pleasures. But, as he gets older and the wars of violent feelings and desires somewhat die down, this is his way of living: he puts his different pleasures on an equal footing and lets himself be ruled by any pleasure which chance puts in his way, turning to another when the first is ended—being against none of them, but nursing them all.

ADEIMANTUS. I see.

SOCRATES. And whenever someone says to him that some pleasures have to do with desires which are good and to be respected, others with ill desires, and that the first are to be kept up and the last put down and made into slaves, he shakes his head and goes on saying that all desires are the same and to be equally respected.

ADEIMANTUS. Yes, that is just what he does.

SOCRATES. So he goes on, living from day to day till the end, pleasuring the chance desire—now drinking himself out of his senses to the sound of music and presently putting himself into hard training; sometimes doing nothing and letting everything go, and then seeming to work like a philosopher. And frequently he takes a part in public business and jumps up and says and does whatever comes into his head. Now he copies some great soldier, hoping to be like him, and next it's a businessman whose part he plays. There is neither law nor order in his days; but this he says is the pleasure-giving, and the free, and the happy way of living, and to it he keeps to the end.

ADEIMANTUS. Well, that is certainly a man whose watchword is 'Free and Equal'.

SOCRATES. Well then, may we put this man by the side (562) of democracy and rightly say he is democratic?

ADEIMANTUS. Be it so!

SOCRATES. Now, we have only to give our account of the most beautiful of all states and the most beautiful of men: that is to say, tyranny and the tyrant.

ADEIMANTUS. Right.

SOCRATES. Come then, my friend, and say how tyranny comes about; that it's an outgrowth from democracy is all but certain. And the change is like the change from plutocracy to democracy.

ADEIMANTUS. How is that?

SOCRATES. Plutocracy thought the good was wealth, didn't it? And the fact that it had no respect for anything else was its destruction. Democracy, too, comes to its end through *its* idea of the good.

ADEIMANTUS. And what is that?

SOCRATES. Freedom. In a democracy they all say that they alone know how to be free and that their state is the only one to live in for the man who is naturally free.

ADEIMANTUS. Why yes, that sort of thing is in everyone's mouth.

SOCRATES. And they call those who support the government 'willing slaves' and 'good-for-nothings'; but praise to the skies any rulers who go about like servants or subjects who behave like kings. In such a state doesn't freedom go beyond limits? Doesn't it get secretly into private houses and go out on every side till at last it takes root among the very animals?

ADEIMANTUS. What *are* you saying now?

SOCRATES. For example, a father tries to seem like a child and lives in fear of his sons; and a son goes (563) on like a father and no longer has any respect for or fear of his father or mother—all to make it clear that he is free—and the stranger sees himself as the equal of the citizen. And the schoolteacher, under these conditions, is in fear of the children and has a great desire to please them, and so it's not surprising if they look down on their teachers and pay no attention. And in general the young copy their elders and compete with them in talk and acts, and the old in turn come down so far as to be running over with bright sayings, copying the young, in order not to seem responsible or like people in authority.

ADEIMANTUS. That's it.

SOCRATES. But the very limit, my friend, is only seen when the men and women slaves are as free as their owners. And I almost overlooked the lengths this goes to in the relations between men and women. So, too, you'll never believe, without in fact experiencing it, how much freer the animals of the house and farm are under this government than under any other. The dog, as the saying goes, becomes like the woman of the house; and in fact even horses and donkeys take on a gait that is strangely free and high-minded, and, on meeting anyone in the street, they run into him if he does not get out of their way, and all the rest are bursting with freedom.

ADEIMANTUS. It is my very notes you are putting before me. All this often takes place when I go into the country!

SOCRATES. Now, from all this the souls of the citizens become so soft and delicate that they grow hot and angry at the least sign that they are not completely free. In the end they make light of the very laws themselves, in order, as they say, not to have the shadow of anyone over them. This then, my friend, if I'm not wrong, is the start, so bright and forceful, out of which tyranny comes. And so, from the highest degree of freedom we go over into the lowest sort of slavery. And the disease which is its root was the increase of men without work in the society. We compared them to drones, (564) some with stings and some without. Now having these two sorts of men in a state is a certain cause of trouble. So any good doctor or law-maker, like a wise keeper of bees, will take steps to keep them from coming into being; or, if they do come, he will get to work as quickly as possible cutting them and their cells out together.

ADEIMANTUS. By Zeus, he will.

SOCRATES. There are three sorts of people in a democracy. These drones are one of them and they are much worse than in a plutocracy, where they are looked down on and kept out of office. For in a democracy they make up the only sort of government body there is. Its sharpest men are always talking and acting, while the rest buzz round and won't let anything else be said. And the next class are the money-makers; and it's from them that the drones get their honey.

ADEIMANTUS. Why, yes, there's no honey to be got from the poor.

SOCRATES. The third sort will be those who work with (565) their hands, and they have nothing to do with politics, and are mostly poor. And this class in a democracy is much the greatest and the most important when it's united.

ADEIMANTUS. But it will only unite to get its part of the honey!

SOCRATES. And it does get a part, but its leaders are good hands at keeping the greater part for themselves. The property owners, after their losses, are forced into taking steps, by arguments at public meetings and whatever else they are able to do.

ADEIMANTUS. Naturally.

SOCRATES. And for this, even if they have no desire for any violent changes, they are said to be plotting against the people, and to be oligarchs. And in the end, when they see that the people, through not knowing enough of the facts, and through propaganda, are bent on wronging them, they do become oligarchs in fact, whether they desire it or not. And so we have division, and charges and trials and attacks made by one side against the other. And the people put up a representative to take care of their cause, a representative they make into a great man. And whenever a tyrant comes into existence,

to judge in this way, and have in the past lived with tyrants, and so can report?

GLAUCON. Certainly.

SOCRATES. Compare now the city and the man. Would you say the tyrant's city is enslaved?

GLAUCON. It is.

SOCRATES. And the tyrannical man, is he enslaved too?

GLAUCON. Enslaved too.

SOCRATES. The city *and* the man, don't they, least of all, do what they truly desire, being always in the power of mad masters?

GLAUCON. It is so.

SOCRATES. And it is for these reasons you would say that this city and this man are the unhappiest of all by far?

GLAUCON. By far.

SOCRATES. As to the tyrannical man, I don't agree.

GLAUCON. Why not?

SOCRATES. Because there is an unhappier man, a tyrannical man who is able really to become an actual tyrant ruling a state.

GLAUCON. Maybe that is so.

SOCRATES. 'Maybe' isn't enough here. We are looking into the most important question there is: the good life and the bad.

GLAUCON. Yes, that is right.

SOCRATES. Take wealthy citizens who own many slaves, do they fear them?

GLAUCON. Why should they?

SOCRATES. Why not?

GLAUCON. Because everybody in the state is ready to defend any of them.

SOCRATES. That's it. But if some god took up a man who owns, say, fifty slaves and put him down, with his wife and children and all his slaves, in some place where no free man could come to help him. What then? What about (579) his fear then?

GLAUCON. The greatest in the world.

SOCRATES. Wouldn't he have to make up to some of his slaves at once, promising them everything and freeing them—though there was nothing he less wanted to do?

GLAUCON. He would, if he didn't want to die.

SOCRATES. And how if the god now gave him neighbours who would not let any man own another, but would be ready to punish any slave-owner to the limit?

GLAUCON. He'd be in a worse position still: nothing but enemies around him.

SOCRATES. And isn't it in that sort of a prison that the actual ruling tyrant finds himself? He, who wants everything, is the only man in the city who cannot travel about or go to the festivals that everyone wants to see, but is forced to spend his time shut up and in fear in the innermost parts of his house—like a woman—envying all the other citizens who can go about wherever they like and see what they will. So isn't an actual ruling tyrant even more unhappy than a private citizen with a tyrannical mind?

GLAUCON. He is indeed.

SOCRATES. Our first argument to show that the soul with a tyrant in it is the unhappiest has been its likeness to a (580) state ruled by a tyrant: enslaved, unable to do anything it really wants to do, poor, in need, afraid, and mad. Here is a second. Parallel to the three classes in a state are the three sides of the soul. And these three sides have three different sorts of pleasures and desires and controls.

GLAUCON. What is all this?

SOCRATES. One side, we say, is that with which a man learns and one is that with which he is angry. But the third side has such numbers of different forms that it was hard to give it any one special name. We named it 'desire' because the desires that have to do with food and drink and love are so strong—and we put the money-loving (581) part with them because money is the chief instrument of such desires. How about naming all these together 'the profit-loving side'? And again, as to the spirited side, because it loves to overcome and to get honour, may we name it 'the honour-loving side'?

GLAUCON. Certainly.

SOCRATES. The first is 'the philosophic side'. What rules men's souls is, with some people, this, and, with others, one of the other two. And that is why we say there are three chief sorts of man—the philosopher or lover of wisdom, the lover of honour, and the lover of profit.

GLAUCON. That is so.

SOCRATES. And there are equally three forms of pleasure parallel to these.

GLAUCON. Certainly.

SOCRATES. And you see, don't you, that if you were to question men of these three sorts in turn, as to which of their lives has the most pleasure in it, each would say that his own was best? The money-maker will say that in comparison with profit the pleasures of honour or of learning are of no value—if they don't produce money. And won't the lover of honour think the pleasure which comes from money is common and low, and that of learning, when it gives no honour, is only smoke and nonsense? And what will the philosopher say of the other pleasures by the side of his delights? Won't he say they are only forced pleasures, because he would have no use for them, if he did not have to have them? Now, how are we to (582) be certain which of them is right about these pleasures?

GLAUCON. I am not able to say.

SOCRATES. Well, what is anything to be judged by if not by experience, reasoning, and discussion? Or will someone name better tests than these?

GLAUCON. No one will.

SOCRATES. See now. Of our three sorts of men, which has had most experience of all these pleasures? Has the lover of profit —by looking into the very being of truth—got more experience of the pleasure which knowledge gives than the philosopher has of the pleasures of profit?

GLAUCON. No, he need know nothing about it. But the philosopher has anyhow to taste the other two pleasures: those of honour and profit, from his earliest days.

SOCRATES. The lover of wisdom, then, has far more experience of both sorts of pleasure. And how is he placed as to the lover of honour?

GLAUCON. Honour, if they succeed, comes to them all, so all are experienced in the sort of pleasure which comes from being respected. But only the lover of wisdom can taste to the full the delight which comes from seeing true being.

SOCRATES. Then, as far as experience goes, he is the best judge of the three.

GLAUCON. By far.

SOCRATES. And he is the only one in whom experience has gone together with reasoning. And again the instrument with which he judges is the instrument not of the lover of profit or honour, but of the philosopher. So, since (583) the tests are experience and wisdom and discussion, it is most true that the pleasure of the part of the soul which learns is the sweetest and the life of the man in whom that part rules has the greatest amount of pleasure in it.

GLAUCON. So the reasoning man at least has authority when he praises his own life.

SOCRATES. And what life and what sort of pleasure come second?

GLAUCON. Clearly the honour-loving life, for it is nearer to the first than the money-maker's is.

SOCRATES. So the lover of profit is in the last place?

GLAUCON. Certainly.

SOCRATES. Then the just man has overthrown the unjust in these two arguments. Now for the third round which gives the decision. Note that pleasures other than those of the mind are not truly pleasure—but a sort of scene-painting, as some wise man has said. Pleasure and pain are opposites, we say. And there is a condition in between them, a sort of rest in the soul. Men who are ill say there is nothing sweeter than to be well—though, before they were ill, they did not know that. And men in great pain say there is no greater pleasure than the end of the pain. And again, when delight comes to an end, that may be painful. But pleasure and pain are a sort of motion in the soul, and this in-between state, (584–5) which is both and neither at once, is a sort of rest. It seems then that these contrast effects are no true pains or pleasures but illusions. But pleasures themselves are a sort of fulfilling—whether they are the pleasures of food for the body or of knowledge for the soul. Which, then, is most fulfilled with that which most truly is—the body with things which are always changing or the soul with that which is ever the same? Which pleasures then will be most real? And the same question must be answered in the same way for the spirited lover of honour as for those who seek only the delights of the body, if they seek their ends apart from reason.

GLAUCON. Yes, that must be so.

SOCRATES. Then we may be certain that the desires (586) which are guided by knowledge and reason, and which seek only those pleasures which have reason's approval, will have the truest pleasures, those right for them and their own—for what is best for anything is what is most its 'own'!

GLAUCON. Yes, that is truly its very own.

SOCRATES. Then when the whole soul takes the wisdom-loving part as its guide without being broken up into (587–8) divisions, each part keeps to its own work in all respects and so is just. Each then delights in its own right pleasures.

GLAUCON. It is so.

SOCRATES. But when one of the other two parts becomes master, the outcome is that it does not get its own pleasure and it forces the others to go after pleasures strange to them and not the true ones. And now let us make an image of the soul, so that those who praise injustice may see clearly what they are saying.

GLAUCON. What sort of an image?

SOCRATES. One of these beings which the old stories are about, a sort of Chimaera, or Scylla, or Cerberus. Make up, then, a Many-headed beast with a ring of heads of tame or violent beasts, and let it be able to change them and cause all sorts of such growths to come out from itself.

GLAUCON. That is hard to do, but language is softer than wax, so we will say it is done.

SOCRATES. Now make a second form like a Lion, and a third like a Man. And let the Many-headed beast be by far the greatest and the Lion smaller.

GLAUCON. That is not so hard; I have done it.

SOCRATES. Join the three in one, and let them seem from without like a man, so that to anyone who can't look inside, who only sees the outer skin, it seems to be one living being only, the man.

GLAUCON. I have put his skin round them.

SOCRATES. Now, let us say this to the person who believes that it profits a man to be unjust and that being just gives him no profit: You are saying that it profits him to feast (589) the Many-headed beast and the Lion, and to keep the Man in him without food, and to make him so feeble that he is pulled about wherever the other two take him, without attempting to make them friends, but letting them go on fighting and biting and eating up one another.

GLAUCON. Yes, that is what the praise of injustice amounts to.

SOCRATES. And he who says justice is of greater profit will say that all our acts and words should give the Man within us complete control over the rest and make him take care of the Beast with the many heads—like a farmer who cares for his plants and keeps down the weeds. And the Man will make a supporter of the Lion, and, caring for all together, will first make them friendly to one another and to himself and so see to their growth.

GLAUCON. Yes, that is what the man who praises justice means.

SOCRATES. From every point of view, then, the praise of justice is true and the praise of injustice false and there is no true knowledge of what he is attacking in the man who is against justice.

GLAUCON. None whatever.

SOCRATES. May we not change his view for him then—for he is not willingly wrong—by saying: Friend, are not the things that are accounted beautiful and ugly by law and custom accounted so for this reason: the beautiful and honoured things help the Man in us (or it may be the godlike in us) to control the Many-headed beast? But the ugly and low things hand the Man over to the Beast.

GLAUCON. He will agree, if I may speak for him.

SOCRATES. What will it profit a man to take gold unjustly if by so doing he makes the best part of him slave to the worst? If his taking the gold made slaves of his son and daughter—slaves to cruel and evil men—would that profit him, however large the sum? So too when giving the Beast his way turns the Lion into a monkey!

GLAUCON. Yes, tell him that.

SOCRATES. Only when a man is too feeble to control (590) the Beasts but has to work for them and please them, only then do we say that he had better be slave to some other man, a man in whom a godlike wisdom rules. And this is to give him the same sort of government. It isn't, as Thrasymachus thought, ruling him to his own loss. No, the best is for everyone to be ruled by a wise and godlike power, if possible seated in his own heart; if not, let it act upon him from without; in order that we may all be, as far as possible, like one another and friends, being all guided by the same pilot.

GLAUCON. Yes, that is right.

SOCRATES. And this is clearly the purpose of law, which (591) is the friend of all the citizens in the state. And it is the purpose of all government of the young, which keeps them from being free till we have formed a government in them, as in a state, and—out of the best in them through the help of the best in us —we have established in their hearts a guardian and ruler— the very same that is in us—from which time they may go free.

GLAUCON. Yes, that is clear.

SOCRATES. The wise man will give all his powers, all his days, to making the state in his soul more just, more temperate, and more wise, and give the highest place to whatever will make it so. And as to the outcome of it all in the opinions others form of him, and the rewards and honours they offer him, he will keep the same measure before his eyes, and prize only what will make him a better man. In (592) public and private life he will put aside all that might overturn the constitution of his soul.

GLAUCON. If that is his chief interest, then I take it he will have no hand in politics.

SOCRATES. Yes, by the dog, he certainly will. At least in his own state, though maybe not in the land of his birth—unless some god-sent chance makes this possible.

GLAUCON. I see. He will take a part, you are saying, in the state we have been founding: a state whose being is in ideas only, for I do not believe it can have any existence on earth.

SOCRATES. Well, maybe its pattern is already there in heaven for him to see who so desires; and, seeing it, he makes himself its citizen. And the question of its present or future existence makes no difference. He who sees it will live by its laws and by no other.

GLAUCON. That seems probable.

BOOK X

SOCRATES. Numbers of other reasons make me see how (595) right we were in our organization of the state—especially in what we did about poetry.

GLAUCON. What was that?

SOCRATES. We kept out all poetry of the sort which copies things, and why it is to be kept out is much clearer now that we have separated the different sides of the soul.

GLAUCON. What is your point here?

SOCRATES. Don't give me away to the tragic poets and the other copiers—but that sort of art, I think, damages the mind. The only remedy would be a knowledge of what it really is.

GLAUCON. What makes you say this?

SOCRATES. Let me say it, though the love and respect I have had for Homer from my boyhood would keep the words back. For he was the first teacher from whom all these beautiful things in tragedy have come. Still, let us not honour a man higher than the truth, and so I will say on. What do you think representation is? For I am not quite certain myself what it is attempting to do.

GLAUCON. Is it likely then that I would know?

SOCRATES. I wouldn't be surprised, for frequently the (596) less clear vision sees things before the sharper.

GLAUCON. That is so, but with you present I would not be very ready to say how anything seemed to me. So go on, yourself.

SOCRATES. Let us start as we generally do—with one Idea or Form which covers the many different things to which we give the same name. Any example will do here. Take beds or tables. There are only two Ideas or Forms here—one of a bed, the other of a table.

GLAUCON. Yes.

SOCRATES. Don't we say that the carpenter produces them by

looking at the Form or Idea, and so makes the beds or the tables we use, and the same with other things? Certainly no workman makes the Form itself. How could he?

GLAUCON. In no way.

SOCRATES. Now what name would you give to a workman who makes all the things that all workmen separately make?

GLAUCON. He sounds like a surprisingly able man!

SOCRATES. Wait a bit and you'll say so with more reason. For this same workman not only makes all sorts of tools but all plants and animals and himself as well, and earth and heaven and the gods and all things in heaven and in Hades under the earth.

GLAUCON. What a sophist!

SOCRATES. You don't believe in him. Is he quite impossible or might there be such a maker who does make all these things in one sense, though in another he doesn't?

GLAUCON. In what way?

SOCRATES. There is nothing hard about it. You may do it yourself and most quickly by taking a looking-glass about with you everywhere. That will quickly produce the sun and all the other things of which we were talking.

GLAUCON. Yes, images of them, but not the things themselves in their own being.

SOCRATES. Good, and that is the point. A painter is this sort of producer. You will say that his works are not real. But still there is a sense in which a painter makes a bed.

GLAUCON. Yes, but it is a pictured bed only.

SOCRATES. But what of the workman who makes beds in (597) fact? We agreed that he does not make the Idea or Form which is the true bed—the bed in itself—but only an example of a bed. But if he doesn't make what truly is, he only makes something which is *like* a true being. It's not true that he makes beings in the complete sense.

GLAUCON. That is what those who are good at this sort of thing say.

SOCRATES. Don't let us be surprised if even this carpenter's bed is again only a shadow in comparison with the true bed.

GLAUCON. No, we will not.

SOCRATES. But let us use this example in looking for what this copier truly is. We get three beds: one which has true being—I take it, God produces that one; one which the workman made; and one which the painter made. Is that so?

GLAUCON. Be it so.

SOCRATES. The painter, the workman, and God, then, are responsible for these three sorts of beds. Now God—because he so willed, or was somehow forced to—made only one true bed. There is only one, for if he were to make two, there would again have to be a Form or Idea they would share as beds and *that* would be the true bed.

GLAUCON. Right.

SOCRATES. And the workman makes everyday beds. But the painter doesn't make and produce that sort of bed.

GLAUCON. Not at all. He's a copier of the things which the others produce.

SOCRATES. Very good. Then a copier is a man who makes what is three steps down from true being.

GLAUCON. Certainly.

SOCRATES. And the tragic poet is a copier too, and, like all artists, three moves away from true being.

GLAUCON. So it seems.

SOCRATES. Then we are in agreement about the copier. (598) But about painting now—does it copy the thing itself or the things the workman makes?

GLAUCON. The last.

SOCRATES. As they are or as they seem to be? Make that clear.

GLAUCON. What is this?

SOCRATES. You may look at a bed from different points of view, straight or sideways, or from any other angle, and the bed will seem different, but it is the same in fact. And so with other things.

GLAUCON. That is so. It seems different but is the same.

SOCRATES. Now take this point. What is painting attempting to do: to copy things as they are or as they seem, the image or what is true?

GLAUCON. The image.

SOCRATES. Then copying is a long way from true being, and that, maybe, is why it is able to produce everything, because it grips only a small part of everything, and that an image. For example: a painter will paint a shoemaker, a carpenter, or any other worker without being master of any of their arts. If he is a good painter, he may take in children or the simple; his picture of a carpenter may make them believe they are truly looking at a carpenter.

GLAUCON. Certainly.

SOCRATES. Well, when they tell us of a man who is an expert in all the arts or say that there is nothing this man doesn't know better than all other men, let us quietly say to ourselves that they are being a little over-ready to believe or have been listening to some wonder-worker or copier and been tricked into believing him all-wise, through not being able to test and separate knowledge, ignorance, and copying.

GLAUCON. Very true.

SOCRATES. Well, don't some people say the tragic poets and Homer, who is at their head, are experts in all the arts and in all things for good and evil which have to do with man, and in all things that are of the gods? The good poet, so they argue, has to make his verses with knowledge or not make them at all. Haven't these people been tricked? Have they noted that copies are three moves away (599) from true things and not hard to produce without any knowledge of what truly is? Or are they right and do good poets in fact have this knowledge about the things they seem to the masses to talk of so well?

GLAUCON. It's a question which has certainly to be looked into.

SOCRATES. If anyone were able to make real things as well as images could he give himself up seriously to image-making?

If he knew the things he copies, he would go in for *them*, not for copying them. He'd hope to be the praised one, not the praiser!

GLAUCON. Yes. The honour is not a bit the same.

SOCRATES. Then let us put a question to Homer—not about medical things or any of the arts his verses only touch on—but about the military arts, and government, and education, which are the chief and noblest things he undertakes to talk of: 'Friend Homer, if you are not three moves away from true being in what you say about virtue, if you are not an image-maker, a copier only, if you *are* able to see what makes men better or worse in public or private life, let us hear what state ever had any better government through your help? The good order of Lacedaemon came from Lycurgus, and other states great and small had other law-makers, but who says you have done them any good? Italy and Sicily say this of Charondas and we of Solon. But who says it of you?' Will he be able to name any?

GLAUCON. No.

SOCRATES. Well then, is there any war on record that (600) was well guided or helped by his orders or suggestions?

GLAUCON. There is not.

SOCRATES. Or any invention, such as might come from an expert in the arts and business of life, from a Thales or Anacharsis?

GLAUCON. Nothing of the sort.

SOCRATES. Well, if Homer never did anything of public note, was he in private a guide or teacher? Had he friends who have handed on a certain Homeric way of life, as with Pythagoras?

GLAUCON. Nothing of that sort is reported.

SOCRATES. But do you take it, Glaucon, that if Homer had in fact been able to give men an education and make them better, and had had true knowledge in place of the art of copying, he wouldn't have had a great following who loved and honoured him? Is it possible that the men of Homer's day, or Hesiod's, would have let Homer and Hesiod go about making songs if they had in fact been able to help men in becoming good? No, they would have held on to *them* and not to their own money. They would have forced them to live with them in their houses, or, if the master wouldn't, they would themselves have gone about with him everywhere till they got enough education.

GLAUCON. Yes, Socrates, that seems quite true.

SOCRATES. Then won't we say that all these poets from Homer down are only copiers; every one of them copies—images of virtue and whatever their verses are about—but never gets to true being? And the people, who know (601) as little and only judge by his words, take it that when he talks of shoemaking or war or what not, in measure and harmony and rhythm, it is all very good—such is the sweet power music and rhythm naturally have. But you have seen again and again that when the musical colouring is taken off them, these sayings by themselves in cold prose don't amount to very much. Maybe you have noted that?

GLAUCON. I have.

SOCRATES. They are like faces which never were truly beautiful, but only young and bright, and that has all gone from them. Here is another point: Take a horse's bit. It is the horseman only who is the truc judge of how to use it, and of its right form. And with everything, aren't there three arts which have to do with it—the user's, the maker's, and the copier's?

GLAUCON. Yes.

SOCRATES. And for everything—for every sort of instrument, living being, or act—doesn't the question 'Is it good, beautiful, right?' come down to the use it is made for or naturally has?

GLAUCON. True.

SOCRATES. The user of anything has the most experience of it and he has to point out to the maker the good and bad effects in use. And so the maker gets his idea of the right and wrong of it from the user, by talking with him (602) and being forced to act on what he has to say. It is the user who has true knowledge.

GLAUCON. Certainly.

SOCRATES. But as the copier hasn't this knowledge and won't take orders from the man who has it, and still will copy, what he copies will probably be the things which seem beautiful to the public—and they don't know.

GLAUCON. That's it.

SOCRATES. Now what is it in men on which this business of copying has such effect?

GLAUCON. What is your point here?

SOCRATES. Something like this: The same size seen from near and from far does not seem the same. The same things seem bent or straight to people who view them in water or out, and hollow or rounded, through the same sort of error in seeing colours. And this way of mixing things up is everywhere in our souls. And scene-painting profits from this, to the point of becoming almost a black art, and so with other conjuring tricks.

GLAUCON. True.

SOCRATES. Don't measuring and numbering and weighing give us most welcome help here? They keep our souls from being overruled by what seems greater or less and hand over the control to what has been numbered, measured, or weighed. And this is the work of the reasoning and thinking part of the soul. And whatever opinions (603) go against this work come from one of the lower things in the soul.

GLAUCON. Necessarily.

SOCRATES. Well, that is my point when I say that the copying arts damage the mind. They produce something far from true and deal with something in us which is far from knowledge and no friend to it for any healthy purpose. And this is true not only with what we see but with verses. So don't let us keep only to this parallel with painting but turn to see if that part of the mind with which poetry in fact deals is good or bad.

GLAUCON. Certainly.

SOCRATES. Poetry copies men: acting either under force or of their own free will; seeing themselves in the outcome to have done well or ill; and, in all this, feeling grief or joy. Is there something in addition?

GLAUCON. Nothing.

SOCRATES. Is a man of one mind with himself in all this? Or is there opposition and fighting with himself—as there was when in vision he had opposite opinions at the same time about the same things? But we agreed on that before. Our souls at any one time are attacked by endless opposite views. There was one thing, however, we didn't say then which has to be said now.

GLAUCON. What is it?

SOCRATES. We said then, I believe, that a good man who is guided by reason will take such blows of fate as the loss of a son or anything very dear to him less hardly than other people.

GLAUCON. Certainly.

SOCRATES. Will he feel no grief or—that being impossible—will he be temperate in his grief?

GLAUCON. The last is truer.

SOCRATES. Will he keep down his grief more when he (604) is under the eyes of his equals or when he is by himself?

GLAUCON. He will be much more self-controlled when he is on view.

SOCRATES. By himself he will cry out, as I see him, in ways which if another heard him would put him to shame, and he'll do things he would not have anyone see him doing. Reason and law urge him to keep down this grief, while the feeling itself forces him to give way to it. So, because there are two opposite impulses in such a man at the same time about the same thing, we say there are two things in him. One of them is ready to be guided by the law which, I take it, says that it is best to keep quiet as far as possible when griefs come and not to cry out, because we are not certain what is good and what is evil in such things, and to take them hardly does not make them any better. Reason says that nothing in man's existence is to be taken so seriously, and our grief keeps us back from the very thing we need as quickly as possible in such times.

GLAUCON. What is that?

SOCRATES. To take thought on the event; and, as we order our play by the way the cards fall, to see how to order our acts, in view of what has come about, in the ways reason points to as the best. Don't let us be like children when they have had a fall, and go on crying out with a hand on the place. Look after the wound first and pick up what has had a fall, and make grief give place to medical help.

GLAUCON. That would certainly be the best way.

SOCRATES. And what is best in us is willing to be guided by reason?

GLAUCON. Clearly.

SOCRATES. And the part which goes over our grief in memory and never has enough of lamenting is unreasoning and useless and feeble-spirited?

GLAUCON. Yes, we will say so.

SOCRATES. Now the part which grieves may be copied in numberless different ways, while the reasoning temperate condition, always nearly the same, is hard to copy or to take in when copied—especially by the masses of very different people who go to the play. That whole way of (605) living is strange to them. The copying poet is not naturally turned toward this best thing in the soul, nor is his art framed to please it, for he has to get the praises of the public. So he gives himself up to the sort of man who cries out in changeful ways as something not so hard to copy. And in doing so he plants an evil government within every soul. He pleases its foolish part. But still we have not come to our chief point against poetry. Its power to make even the better sort of men worse is the thing most to be feared.

GLAUCON. It would be, if poetry could do that.

SOCRATES. Hear and take thought. The very best of us, hearing

Homer or one of the other tragic poets copying some great man in grief, running on and on in his outcries, or wounding himself in his pain, have feelings of pleasure and let our hearts go out to the picture. We give ourselves up to it and praise, as a great poet, whoever makes us do this most.

GLAUCON. We do.

SOCRATES. But in our own lives, when some grief comes upon us, we take pride in the opposite behaviour, in our power to keep quiet and take it with courage, believing that this is a man's part and that the other we were praising in the play is a woman's. Are we right to praise so what we would be ashamed of in ourselves?

GLAUCON. By Zeus, no. There is no reason in that!

SOCRATES. There is if you look at it this way.

GLAUCON. Which way?

SOCRATES. In our own grief there is that in the soul which (606) is kept back by force, which by its very nature is in need of tears and lamentations as an outlet. This is what the poets please and delight in us. And what is best in us, having never had a right education or even training, lets down its guard over this grieving part because here we are looking on at the grief of others. But what we take pleasure in when we see it in others will have its effect on ourselves; after feasting our feelings of pity *there* it is hard to keep them down in our own grief. Few are able to see that.

GLAUCON. Most true.

SOCRATES. And it is the same with the causes of laughter, with comedies, or in private talk. When you take the greatest pleasure in things so low that you would be full of shame about them if they were yours, you are doing just what you do at the tragedy. Sometimes you let yourself go so far that before you know it you become a clown yourself in private. And so, again, with the desires of sex, and with anger and all the other passions and desires and pains and pleasures of the soul that go along with all our acts. The effect of such poetry is the same. It waters and cares for these feelings when what we have to do is dry them up. It makes us be ruled by the very things which have to be ruled, if we are to become better and happier men.

GLAUCON. I may not say no.

SOCRATES. Then, Glaucon, when the praisers of Homer say that he was the educator of Hellas, and that if a man is to guide and better his behaviour he will do well to give himself up to reading Homer, and that we are to order (607) our lives by his teaching, we may love and honour these people—as doing their very best—and agree that Homer is the highest and first of all tragic poets; but let us keep true to our belief that only hymns to the gods and praises of good men may be allowed in our state. For if you let in this honey-sweet music, pleasure and pain, not law and what may rightly be thought best, will be its lords.

GLAUCON. Most true.

SOCRATES. So—to make an end of this—we had good cause to send this honeyed Muse out of our state. For reason ordered so. And let us say again, if she protests against us as rough and unlettered, that there has been an old quarrel between poetry and philosophy of which the signs are everywhere. But if poetry has good arguments for a place in a well-ordered state, why then with joy we will let her in, for we ourselves well know the delights she offers. Only we may not sin against what we believe to be true. Is that not so, my friend? You yourself are moved by her, especially when the voice comes through the lips of Homer.

GLAUCON. Very much so.

SOCRATES. We will let her come back if she can make good her defence in any verse she pleases. And we will let her friends—those who are not poets but lovers of poetry—plead her cause in prose, and say, if they can, how she is not only delightful but useful in ordering government and man's life. And with goodwill we will hear them, for it will all be clear profit to us, if truly it is made out that she gives not only pleasure but things of use.

GLAUCON. Certainly we will profit.

SOCRATES. But if it is not so, my friend, as men who have been in love and see that their love is not good for them (608) turn away, however hard it is; so we, though our miseducation has made us love such poetry, still will say these reasons over to ourselves, as a charm to keep ourselves from slipping back under her power into the childlike loves of the masses. For, as we see now, we are not to take such poetry seriously as a thing with truth in its hands. He who gives ear to it must believe what we say and keep watch and fear for his soul's state.

GLAUCON. I am altogether with you.

SOCRATES. Yes, for much turns, dear Glaucon, more than we are conscious of, on a man's becoming good or bad; so never may the attractions of honour or wealth or any office, no not even of poetry, make us careless of justice or of the rest of virtue.

GLAUCON. All we have said makes me agree with you; everyone would, I think.

SOCRATES. But we have still said nothing about the greatest rewards of virtue.

GLAUCON. Can there be other things greater than these we have talked of?

SOCRATES. What great thing may a little time take in? One lifetime is small in comparison with all time.

GLAUCON. It is nothing.

SOCRATES. What then? Should an eternal thing be seriously troubled about anything so short rather than about all time?

GLAUCON. You are right. But why do you say this?

SOCRATES. Have you not seen that our souls live for ever and never come to an end?

GLAUCON. No, by Zeus, I haven't. Are *you* able to say that?

SOCRATES. How would I not? And you may, for there is nothing hard about it.

GLAUCON. There is for me, and I'll be glad to hear this argument you take so lightly.

SOCRATES. Do you agree to this? What damages anything and makes it worse is evil; and what keeps it safe (609) and makes it better is good. And everything has its own special good and its own special evil. And when one of these evils comes to anything it makes this thing it attacks bad, and in the end destroys it.

GLAUCON. It does.

SOCRATES. The point is that the destruction of anything comes from its own natural evil, its own disease, and if that is not able to put an end to it, no other thing may; for clearly the good will not, nor, again, that which is neither good nor bad.

GLAUCON. Certainly not.

SOCRATES. When we see, then, something which has a natural evil which makes it worse, but is *not* able to destroy it, won't we be certain that such a thing will never be broken up or destroyed?

GLAUCON. That seems probable.

SOCRATES. Well, hasn't the soul something which makes it evil?

GLAUCON. Truly it has: all the things we've been going over —injustice and loose ways and the wrong fears and ignorance.

SOCRATES. Does any one of these put an end to it? Take thought, and don't let us be tricked into mistaking the destruction of the body for that of the soul. Note, Glaucon: a body is not broken up by what is bad in its food, whatever that may be, but only when that causes in the body its own evil condition—the disease which is the effect (610) of the bad food. By the same argument, if the evil of the body does not produce in the soul the soul's own evil, the soul will not be broken up or destroyed by any evil which is not its own. The evil of one thing is never the destruction of another.

GLAUCON. That is reasonable.

SOCRATES. Never say, then, that the soul comes to an end by

any disease, or by a knife through the throat, or even when the body is cut into little bits. We have to say that these things don't wound the soul if there is no reason to think that they make the soul itself more unjust.

GLAUCON. No one will argue that men's souls are made more unjust by dying.

SOCRATES. But if anyone is so brave as to come to grips with this argument and say—to get out of being forced to believe that the soul is immortal—that at death a man does become more evil and unjust, we will say that, if so, injustice would be a disease which put its victim to death and the more quickly the more unjust he was. But in fact, when the unjust are killed, they come to their bodily end—*because* of their injustice, no doubt—only *by* the acts of those who punish them.

GLAUCON. By Zeus, injustice would not be so much to be feared after all, if it caused the death of the evildoer, for that would be a way out of all troubles. But it seems to me injustice is quite the opposite; it may put others to death when it is able to, but, so far from killing the illdoer, it makes him livelier and more wideawake than before.

SOCRATES. Well said. Then there is no one evil, its own (611) or another's, which puts an end to the soul. So it lives forever.

GLAUCON. Necessarily.

SOCRATES. But, if so, the number of souls will always be the same. Increase would come from the mortal and all things would end by becoming eternal. We will not say so, for the argument will not let us. And again, we may not say that in its truest being the soul is the sort of thing which is full of very different, contradictory, and opposite things—as we have been saying it is.

GLAUCON. What is this?

SOCRATES. What is immortal may not well be made up of numbers of things not put together in the best way.

GLAUCON. It is improbable.

SOCRATES. But the argument we have just gone through, and

other reasons, force us to the decision that the soul is immortal. To see what it truly is, you must view it not as now spotted by keeping company with the body and other evils, but judge rightly, in the light of reason, what it is when it is cleared of all this—and then you will see it to be a far more beautiful thing and will more clearly separate justice from injustice and understand all the rest that our discussion has been about. We have been talking of how it seems to us at present. We have been looking on the soul as men did on the sea-god Glaucus. What he was might hardly be made out because his arms and legs were broken off and cut and crushed by the waves, and he was coated over with shells and sea plants and stones so that, to look at, he might have been any sort of beast in place of what he truly was. So do we see the soul, lowered to this condition by unnumbered evils. But let us turn our eyes another way, Glaucon.

GLAUCON. Where?

SOCRATES. To its love of wisdom. And note the things it has a care for and the company it desires—being itself of the same family with the godlike, the ever-living, and the eternal. Take thought, then, how the soul might be if it went after this without hanging back, and by this impulse were taken up out of this deep sea in which it is (612) now, and were cleaned and freed from the stones and shellfish which now cover it over so thickly with a stony and earthy coat because of its feasts here below, which are taken to be so happy. Then would we see what it truly is in itself, if complex or simple, one or more than one, and what is true of it and how. But for now we have given enough of an account of what it undergoes and of the forms it takes on in this present life of ours.

GLAUCON. We have, certainly.

SOCRATES. The other conditions of the argument we have kept as well. And we haven't talked of the rewards and fair name of justice—as you said Homer and Hesiod do—but we have made it clear that justice in itself is the best thing for the soul itself, and that the soul will do well to be just even if it has Gyges's ring.

GLAUCON. Most true.

SOCRATES. Is there anything now, Glaucon, against our letting justice, and virtue generally, have all the different rewards they win for the soul in this life and hereafter?

GLAUCON. Nothing.

SOCRATES. The first thing to give back will be that knowledge which the gods certainly have of the just and the unjust. And all that they send to their friend will be (613) for his good—putting on one side the evil that had to come to him from his sins in an earlier life. Even poverty, disease—or any other thing said to be evil—will to the just in the end be for good in life as in death. For the gods will take care of the man who truly desires to do right and, by doing so, to become as nearly like God as it is possible for a man to be. Such will be his reward from the gods. And what do the just get from men? What does in fact take place? The unjust start off well in the race but don't get back from the turn. Those wicked men are quick enough at first, but in the end how foolish they look, creeping off the field, uncrowned, with their ears hanging down on their necks. But the true runners, when they come to the end, get the prizes and are crowned. And that is so, as a rule, with the just, isn't it; toward the end of every act and undertaking and of life itself they have honour and praise from men?

GLAUCON. It is so.

SOCRATES. May I not say of them what you said of the unjust? I am going to say that the just, when they become older, get positions in the government if they will, have their children married into whatever families they please . . . every other thing you said of the one I will say of the other. And of the unjust in turn I will say that most of them—even if they are not seen through at first—are caught in the end. They undergo all the things you truly said were not for gentle ears. Take it I've gone through all that. Well? May I say that?

GLAUCON. Certainly, for it is just.

SOCRATES. While he lives such are the rewards of the (614) just man from gods and men—in addition to the blessings of Justice herself.

GLAUCON. Fair and lasting rewards.

SOCRATES. But nothing in number or amount to those waiting for him after death. Give ear, then, to a story about them so that just and unjust both may get in full all that was to be said of them in our argument.

GLAUCON. Say on. There is little that I would more gladly hear.

SOCRATES. This is not the story Alcinous heard, but the story of a brave man, Er, the son of Armenius, a Pamphylian by birth. It came about that, after falling in battle, his body was taken up on the tenth day, unchanged, and on the twelfth day, when his body was stretched on the wood ready to be burned, he came back to life, and he gave this account of what he had seen over there on the other side. He said that when his soul went out of his body, he journeyed in company with a great band of others till they came to a strange place, where two openings side by side in the earth faced two others in the heavens. Between them were judges who fixed on the just a sign of their reward in front and on the backs of the unjust an account of their crimes, and the just they sent up through the heaven on the right hand and the unjust down by the lower way on the left. When Er came before them himself, they said that he was to be a witness to men to report to them of that other world, and they ordered him to watch and hear everything in that place. Then he saw the souls after judgement going off by one of the openings of heaven and one of earth, while by the other two openings other souls were coming back, dirty and covered with dust from under earth, or clean and shining from heaven. They kept coming back as if from a long journey, and gladly took up their places on the field as persons do at some great festival. Friends welcomed one another, and those from within the earth asked about the heaven, and (615) in turn were questioned about the life under earth. And these wept and cried out at the memory of all the things they had seen and undergone in their journey down under the earth—and it went on a thousand years—while those from the heaven talked of joys and visions of things more beautiful than any words might picture. The full story, Glaucon, would take us over-long, but this, Er said, was the substance. For every wrong they had done to others, they made a payment ten times as great; and this was measured in periods of a hundred years, for a human life was taken to be a hundred years long, so that they had ten punishments for every crime; and again those who had done good acts, and been just and holy men, had their reward in the same measure. And there were rewards and punishments still greater for those who were pious or impious to their parents or to the gods, or who put themselves to death. He was within hearing when one was questioned by another, 'Where is Ardiaeos the Great?' Now this Ardiaeos had been ruler in a town of Pamphylia a thousand years before that time, and had put to death his old father and a brother older than himself, and had done numbers of other unholy things. And the other answered, 'He has not come, and probably will never come. For this was one of the fearful things we saw. When we were near the mouth, and were able to come out, and all our other pains were ended, we suddenly saw him with others, most of them tyrants, though some were private persons who had done great wrongs. And when these were about to go up and out, the mouth would not take them, but roared when any of those who were too evil to be reformed, or who had not completed their punishment, attempted to come up. And then', he said, 'violent men, like fire to look at, who heard the Voice, would seize them and take them off; and Ardiaeos and others they took and knotted (616) with cords, head and hand and foot, and dragged them by the wayside, combing them with thorns, like wool, and saying to those who went by why this was and that they were to be thrown into Tartarus.' And then, of all they had undergone this fear was the worst for each—that the mouth would roar when he attempted to go up, and everyone went up most gladly when the Voice was quiet. These, said Er, were among the pains and punishments, and there were rewards as great.

Now when they had been in the green field seven days, they were forced to journey on, and they came in four days to a place where they saw, stretching from on high through the heaven and the earth, a straight line like a pillar, and like the rainbow, but brighter and clearer. They came to this after another day's journey, and there at the middle of the light they saw the ends of its chains stretching from heaven; for this light was the band which keeps the spinning heavens together, like the bands about a ship. And from the ends was stretched the spindle of Necessity, on which all the circles turn. Its rod and hook were made of steel, and the whorl upon it was made of steel and other materials. And the form of the whorl was like those used on the earth: from his account there seems to be one great hollow whorl, and another within it, like boxes which go inside one another, and in the same way a third, a fourth, and four others, for there were eight of the whorls in all, one within another, their edges seeming like circles from the upper side, but together they form the back of one solid whorl about the rod, which is fixed right through the middle of the eighth. The first and outermost whorl has the widest edge, the sixth has the second widest, then the fourth, then the eighth, then the seventh, then the fifth, then the third, and the second has the narrowest edge. The edge of the greatest whorl is of mixed colours; that of the seventh is brightest; that of the eighth takes it colour from the (617) seventh shining upon it. The colours of the second and fifth are like one another, being warmer than the seventh and eighth. The third is whitest, the fourth is a little red, and the sixth is the second whitest. The whole spindle turns one way, but within the unit as it turns the seven inner circles turn gently in the opposite direction, and of these seven the eighth moves most quickly, and after it the seventh, sixth, and fifth move together, and more slowly turns the fourth as it seemed, moving back upon itself, and then the third, and the fifth and slowest motion is that of the second. And the spindle turns round upon the knees of Necessity. On every one of its circles is a Siren, who travels round with the circle, and cries out on one note, and the eight notes are joined in one harmony. And round about are seated at equal distances the Fates, the daughters of Necessity, Lachesis, Clotho and Atropos; who, clothed in white robes, with flowers on their heads, keep harmony in their song with the music of the Sirens. And the song of Lachesis is of the past; that of Clotho, of the present; that of Atropos, of the future. And Clotho with her right hand helps to turn the outer edge of the whorl, stopping from time to time, and Atropos with her left hand turns the inner circles, while Lachesis in turn helps one or the other.

Now, coming here, the souls were sent before Lachesis, and first a sort of prophet placed them in order and, having taken from the knees of Lachesis certain lots and designs of lives, went up to a high pulpit and said, 'The word of Lachesis, daughter of Necessity: Souls that live for a day, here is the start of another round taking men back to death. Your daimon will not be given you by chance but will be of your own choosing. Let him who gets the first lot choose the life he wills, which then shall be his destiny. But Virtue is free; a man will have more or less of her, as he honours her or not. He who chooses is responsible, Heaven is guiltless.' Having said this, he cast the lots down among them all, and every soul took up the lot that fell to him, all but Er, who was ordered not to do so. After this the prophet placed designs (618) of lives before them on the earth, and they were far greater in number than the company. They were of every sort, for there were lives of all sorts of animals and all sorts of men, there were tyrannies among them, some unbroken till the end, and others cut short and changing into poverty, beggardom and exile. And there were lives of men noted for their beautiful forms and faces and strength as athletes, or for their high birth and the virtues of their fathers, and lives of the opposite sorts; and of women the same. But quality of soul was not fixed in them, because a soul taking up a different life necessarily becomes different. But all other things were mixed with one another, and with riches and poverty, disease and strength, and the middle ways between them.

There, my dear Glaucon, is *the* danger of dangers for every man. That is why every one of us—putting all other cares on one side—has to look for the man who will give him the power and the knowledge to separate the life which is good from that which is bad, and always and everywhere to make the best decision which conditions offer him. And let him take into account all the things we have talked of, and see how the quality of his life will be changed by their being present or not present in it. Let him judge the effects of high and low birth, private station and office, of being strong or feeble, quick or slow, and all such gifts of the soul, natural or gained by experience, when mixed and joined with one another; so that by weighing all these things he will be able to make a reasonable decision between better and worse lives, with his eyes fixed on the innermost being of the soul, naming as worse a life which will have a tendency to make it more unjust, and as better one which will make it more just. But all other thoughts he will let be, for we have seen that this is the choice of all choices, for life and for death. A man needs to (619) take with him to the house of death an adamantine faith in this, so that even there he may not be dazzled by wealth and other waste, and jump into tyrannies and suchlike crimes, and so do evil which can never be put right, and undergo still greater himself; but may always be able to judge and take the life which is in the middle way, and keep from excess in this direction or that, in this life so far as may be and in the life to come; for this is man's greatest happiness.

Moreover, the witness from the other side reported that the prophet then said: 'Even he who comes forward last, if he chooses wisely, and lives hard and seriously, will get a good enough life, not an evil one. Let not the first make his choice without care, or the last be downhearted.' When the prophet had said these things, the one who had the first number jumped at once for the greatest tyranny, and in his foolish greed he took it without examination, not seeing that he was fated by it to eat his own children, and other shocking things. And when he read it through, he hammered his breast and lamented over his choice, without recalling what the prophet had said. He did not look upon himself as responsible, but cried out against chance and the gods and anything but himself. He was one of those who had come from heaven, a man who had lived under a well-ordered government, and so had gained some measure of virtue by use, and not by philosophy. It seems that of those who were thus overtaken, not a few came from heaven; they had not been schooled by trouble. For most of those who came from under earth did not choose carelessly, for they had undergone pain themselves, and had seen the pains of others. For which reason as well as through the chances in the lots there was generally an exchange of the good and bad. But if, whenever he comes back to the life of this earth, a man loves wisdom and does not get one of the very last numbers, by this report he will not only be happy here, but his journey back to this world will not be rough and under the earth, but smooth and through the heavens. More than strange it was, (620) he said, how the different souls chose their lives—sad and absurd, and foolish, for their choice was guided for the most part by what they were used to in their earlier lives. He saw the soul of Orpheus, he said, choose the life of a swan, for he hated all women because of his death at their hands, and was unwilling to have a woman give him birth. He saw the soul of Thamyris choosing the life of a nightingale, and a swan changing over to the life of man, and the same with other music-making animals. The soul which had the twentieth number took the life of a lion; it was the soul of Ajax, the son of Telamon, which, remembering the decision as to the arms of Achilles, was unwilling to become a man. The one after, the soul of Agamemnon, for the same reason that its pains had made it hate all men, changed to the life of an eagle. The soul of Atalanta gave one look at the great honours of an athlete's life and grasped them at once, unable to go farther. After her, he said, he saw the soul of Epeius, the son of Panopeus, taking on the nature of an expert workwoman. Far off at the back the soul of the clown Thersites was putting on the body of an ape. And it chanced that the soul of Odysseus had the last number of all, and came to make its selection. From memory of the toils of its last life, it had no longer any ambition, and went about everywhere in search of the quiet life of a private person, and was a long time looking till it saw it at last in some out-of-the-way place untouched by the others, and, on seeing it, said that it would have done the same if it had had the first number, and took it gladly. And in the same way with the rest: beasts changed into men and into one another, the unjust into cruel beasts, the just to gentle ones, and there were mixtures of all sorts. But now, when all the souls had chosen lives in the order of their numbers, they were taken in turn before Lachesis. And she sent with every one the daimon he had chosen to guide his life and see that all came true. And this guide first took the soul to Clotho, under the twisting motion of her hand, and so fixed the destiny he had chosen. After touching her, the daimon took the soul to the turning hand of Atropos, that the threads might never be untwisted. From there, the souls travelled without turning back under the throne (621) of Necessity. When all had passed, they journeyed into the Levels of Oblivion, through thick, painful heat, for there were no trees or plants; and in the evening they stopped by the River of Unmindfulness whose water no vessel may keep. They were all made to take a measure of the water; those who were not saved by their good sense drank more than the measure, so that all memory of everything went from them. And after they had gone to sleep and it was the middle of the night, there was a sound of thunder and a shaking of the earth, and they were suddenly sent away, one this way, one that, up to their birth, like quickly moving stars. Er himself, he said, was kept from drinking the water; but he had no idea how and in what way he went back to his body. Only he suddenly opened his eyes at dawn, and saw himself stretched on a funeral pyre.

And so, Glaucon, the story was saved, and will save us, if we believe it; we will pass safely across the River of Lethe, and keep our souls clean. If you will be guided by me, we will believe that the soul lives forever, and is able to undergo every measure of good and evil. We will keep ever to the upward road, and follow justice and reason always and in every way, that we may be friends to ourselves and to the gods, both while we are here and when, like victors in the games, we have our reward. And so, here on earth and in that journey of a thousand years, it will be well with us.